Notes on
American
Government

Second Edition

MANOUTCHEHR M. ESKANDARI-QAJAR, PH. D.
Santa Barbara City College

KENDALL/HUNT PUBLISHING COMPANY
4050 Westmark Drive   Dubuque, Iowa 52002

To Fariba, Amir and Yassi,

with extreme prejudice

Contents

Preface vii

Outline of Themes ix

Introduction xvii

Definitions xxiii

PART I: THEORY

CHAPTER 1 Democracy 3

CHAPTER 2 Models of Democracy 7

CHAPTER 3 The Model of the Political System 11

CHAPTER 4 Parliamentary, Presidential and Hybrid Forms of Government 15

CHAPTER 5 Territorial Divisions in Democracies 19

PART II: PROCESS

CHAPTER 6 Documents of Democracy 23

CHAPTER 7 Principles of the U.S. Constitution 27

CHAPTER 8 Socialization, Political Opinion and Participation 37

CHAPTER 9 Electoral Politics, Electoral Systems, and the Electoral College 43

PART II: INSTITUTIONS

CHAPTER 10 Interest Groups and Political Parties 55

CHAPTER 11 Congress: The Legislative Branch 61

CHAPTER 12 Legislative Role of the President 67

CHAPTER 13 The Presidency 71

CHAPTER 14 The Judicial Branch 79

CHAPTER 15 Civil Rights and Civil Liberties 83

APPENDIX

APPENDIX A The Modified Almond and Powell Model of the Political System 89

APPENDIX B The Declaration of Independence (1776) 91

APPENDIX C   Federalist 10 (1787) 93

APPENDIX D   Federalist 51 (1788) 101

APPENDIX E   *Marbury v. Madison* (1803) 107

APPENDIX F   *McCulloch v. Maryland* (1819) (Excerpts) 115

APPENDIX G   *Barron v. Mayor & City Council of
                   Baltimore* (1833) 117

APPENDIX H   The Gettysburg Address (1863) 121

APPENDIX I   *Plessy v. Ferguson* (1896) 123

APPENDIX J   *Brown v. Board of Education of Topeka,
                   Kansas* (1954) 139

APPENDIX K   The Four Freedoms (1941) (Excerpts) 145

APPENDIX L   How Democratic Is America? 149

APPENDIX M   Does Government Do What People Want? 179

Bibliography 183

 # Preface

This second edition of the collection of notes on the subject of American government is intended to help the student make the most of the lectures and the assigned readings in the textbook(s) and guide the student steadily through the semester, from quiz to exam to paper to the final. These notes can be thought of as the dots the student will connect by means of the explanations in the lectures and the readings to form a complete picture of what the shape and dynamics of the American political system is and what "governing" America entails.

These notes will not parallel assigned readings exactly; there would be no point to that. They will add other dimensions to the discussion that might not have been fully explored in the assigned textbook readings, and they will be the basis for further explorations of topics in the lectures. Though geared to classes taught by the author, they can, nevertheless, be used beneficially in any class on American government, as the subject matter treated in them addresses generally the core themes of any course on American government.

These notes are the result of twenty years of teaching of the subject of American government and have thus evolved over time to incorporate themes that have been found useful for the students' better understanding of the subject matter. They are still, however, in a process of evolution, and each semester and class adds a new dimension to them. Thus, students are encouraged to add their own questions and emphases to what is given here and, if proven useful, will find those emphases in future editions of these notes for the benefit of their peers in those classes. Teaching is as much about "teaching" as it is about "learning." Over the years, students have taught this author a great deal about how to teach better. This evolving process of notes is just one of those examples.

These notes are divided into three sections, paralleling the sections of the course. Part I deals with models and theory of American government. Part II deals with the process of American politics. Part III deals with the institutions in the American political system. This second edition of the notes contains a few additional lectures. It also contains a few "sidebars" at the end of selected lecture notes, addressing current developments and noteworthy points that may not be mentioned in regular textbooks or occur in every political cycle the country undergoes. Examples of such sidebars are the discussions of off-year elections, new executive powers such as the use of signing statements and the notion of a unitary executive, the challenges to the writ of *habeas corpus* that special military commissions pose, the 527 phenomenon, etc.

As with everything else, these notes are not substitutes for serious study habits and effort, nor are they perfectly complete. As a matter of fact, several chapters in the textbook have not been addressed at all in these notes. It will be up to the student to complete whatever is missing here with the help of the assigned readings in the book(s) and the lectures. Any clarifications and questions should also be addressed in office hours with the professor, and where and when available, with visits to tutors or teaching assistants at assigned hours.

 # Outline of Themes

The following is a list of themes discussed in the three parts of the course, leading up to the final examination. At a minimum, students need to be familiar with these concepts to be able to have a chance at answering the quizzes, midterm and final examination questions in the most basic fashion.

PART I: CONCEPTS AND THEORIES

1) Definitions: Democracy; Politics; Political System; Government; Power; etc.

2) Views of Democracy

   Procedural

   Substantive

3) Types of Democracy

   Direct

   Indirect or Representative

       Republics

       Constitutional Monarchies

4) Possible Types of Republics

   Parliamentary

   Presidential

   Hybrid

5) Possible Territorial Divisions in Representative Democracy

   Unitary

   Confederate

   Federal

6) Documents of American Democracy

Magna Carta

Declaration of Independence

Articles of Confederation

U.S. Constitution and the Bill of Rights

7) Principles of the U.S. Constitution

Constitutionalism

Republicanism

Bicameralism

Separation of Powers

Checks and Balances

Federalism

8) Definition, Examples, Phases, and Models of Federalism

Definition: Federalism As a Relationship of Power

Examples

Constitution (Various Articles)

Court Cases

Marbury v. Madison (1803)

McCulloch v. Maryland (1819)

Barron v. Baltimore (1833)

Slaughterhouse Cases (1873)

Phases and Models

Phases

Dual Federalism

Cooperative Federalism

New Federalism (and Variations)

Models

Layer-Cake

Marble-Cake

Picket-Fence

Fiscal Federalism and Revenue Sharing

9) Civil Liberties and Civil Rights

Civil Liberties: The Bill of Rights and Its Meaning

Civil Rights

Nationalizing the Bill of Rights: *Barron v. Baltimore*

Dual Citizenship

14th Amendment

Plessy v. Ferguson (1896)

Reconstruction

Brown v. Board of Education (1954)

Civil Rights Movement

Affirmative Action

Reverse Discrimination: Regents of *U.C. v. Bakke* (1978)

Current Developments

PART II: PROCESS

1) Definitions

Socialization

Political Socialization

Opinion/Political Opinion

Political Participation

2) Discussion: Relationship between Political Socialization →
Political Opinion → Political Participation

3) Agents of Socialization (What the "Environment" Adds)

Family	Peers
Media	"Government" + Political System
School	Religious Institutions
Job	Social Affiliations

4) Factors of Socialization: (What We "Bring to the Table")

The Standard Socioeconomic Model of Participation

Factors

Age	Gender
Race	Education
Marital Status	Income
Region	Religion
Family Background (Social Status)	

5) Political Opinion

Core American Political Values

Liberty

Equality

Order

Justice

Democracy

Separation of Church and State

Prevalent Ideologies

Liberalism

Conservatism

Populism

Libertarianism

Socialism

Others

6) Political Participation

Types of Participation

Conventional/Supportive

Nonparticipation

Unconventional/Nonsupportive

Violent Opposition

Levels of Participation: From Uninterested Observer to Candidate for Office

7) Electoral Politics and Electoral Systems

Electoral Politics   Electoral Systems

    The Census   Unanimity

    Congressional Districts   Majority

    Redistricting   Plurality

    Gerrymandering   Proportional Representation

    Reapportionment   Single-Member Districts

    The Electoral College   Winner-takes-all

Types of Elections

    National   State

        Primaries   Referenda

        Caucuses   Initiatives

        Nominations   Propositions

        General Elections   Ballot Measures

        "Off-year"   Gubernatorial

        "Midterm"   State Legislatures
        (House; 1/3 Senate)

        Presidential   State Judiciaries

    Local

        County Boards of Supervisors

        City Councils

        Mayoral Elections

        Judgeships (Superior Court)

        City and County Officials (Treasurer, Sheriff, District Attorney, etc.)

        Initiatives, Propositions, Ballot Measures

        Special District (Schools, Water, College)

PART III: INSTITUTIONS

1) Modified Almond and Powell Model of the Political System

2) How Do Issues Turn into Policies: Model of the Interaction of "Society" with the Political System (Almond and Powell Model)

   How Do Issues Become "Inputs"

   Role of Interest Groups in the American Political System

   > Linkage Institution

   > Gatekeeper

3) Functions of the Political System and the Institutions within It

   Political System → Socialization, Recruitment, Communication

   Interest Groups → Articulation

   Political Parties → Aggregation

   Government → Legislation, Execution, Adjudication

   Bureaucracy → Implementation

4) Interest Groups

   Types and Focus: Narrow/Single Issue vs. Broad/Multi-Issue

   Functions: "Character of Interest Groups"

   Strategies for Political Power

   "How Interest Groups Influence Congress"

   Theories of Democracy Relating to Interest Groups

   > Pluralism

   > Hyperpluralism

   > Elitism

   Models describing Actual Interest Group Politics

   > Iron Triangles

   > Issue Networks

   Political Action Committees and Campaign Finance Regulations

   > Definition of PACs

   > FEC Rules

   > Hard vs. Soft Money

Campaign Finance Reform: McCain-Feingold (update)

New Development: "527s"

5) Political Parties: Elections and the Role of Parties:

Discussion: Relationship between Electoral Systems and Number of Political Parties

Reasons for "Two-party System" in the American Political System

Role of Parties in National Elections

    Primaries

    Caucuses

    Nominations

    General Elections

    "Midterm" (House; 1/3 Senate)

    Presidential

6) Congress

Article 1 of Constitution

Leadership in Congress

Powers of Congress: Article 1.8

    Enumerated and "Elastic Clause"

    Exclusive Powers of House and Senate: Article 1.2, Art 1.7, Article 1.3, Article 2.2.

Legislative Process: Congress and President (Checks and Balances)

    Article 1.7

7) The Executive Branch

Article 2 of the Constitution

Roles and Powers of the President

Legislative Powers of Presidents

The Executive Office of the President

The Executive Branch

8) The Supreme Court

Article 3 of the Constitution

Nature and Types of Laws

Jurisdictions of the Court

Judicial Review

Decision-making Process of the Court

Examples of famous Court Cases

9) The Bureaucracy

Types of Policies

Distributive

Extractive

Regulatory

Redistributive

Models of Policy-Making

Incrementalism

Public Choice

Rational Decision-Making

Alternative Models

Case Studies

The Budget Process

The War Powers Act (2008)

Others

# **Introduction**

One of the many questions students who enroll in courses in political science have has to do with the scope of the field. Very few first-semester students understand what they can do with a major in political science in real life and what the field itself entails. The following points are meant to give some preliminary answers to this and other related questions students may have, and will focus obviously on American government, since that is the area of emphasis that brought these students, at least, in contact with the larger field of political science.

The subject of American government or American politics is one of the subfields of study in the discipline or "major" of political science at American universities. Elsewhere in the world, "American government" would be studied as part of one of the other subfields of political science called comparative politics, where emphasis would be put on the similarities and differences between the various political systems studied, and the American one would be one of the case studies among others.

In America, however, American government is its own subfield in political science, and as students progress to the upper-division levels of four-year schools, and thence to graduate studies, they realize that the subfield itself divides into further areas of study and specialization such as a study of the presidency, or of the U.S. Congress, or of the Supreme Court or of the Constitution itself exclusively. Other areas of specialization in political science related to the subfield of American government are also, therefore, American political thought, constitutional law, public administration, public policy studies, voting behavior and participation, interest group dynamics and political parties, American foreign policy, and a new field of studies, law and society.

While studies of the presidency, the Congress or the Supreme Court, prepare one specifically for expertise in the institutional dynamics of the American political system as they relate to the three branches of government, public administration and public policy studies complete this institutional inquiry into the American political system by including the bureaucracy and the implementation of decisions by the three branches. Both for those seeking a career in the teaching profession and for those seeking public office or employment in the public sector, these areas of emphasis are crucial in that they provide a complete view of the process of governance in America at the federal, state, and local levels.

For those seeking careers in law, as civil or criminal lawyers, or as constitutional lawyers with aspirations to the highest bench in the land, the U.S. Supreme Court, or as professors of constitutional law, the subfields of U.S. constitutional law and American political thought, as well as the field of law and society are good preparations for those careers. Again, with each level of progress from lower division to upper division to graduate studies, the degree of specialization and refinement of focus differs, so that even within these subfields further areas of specialization can be sought and found, such that students of constitutional law might develop expertise on Fourteenth Amendment issues of equal protection or Fifth Amendment issues of due process exclusively. Other areas of specialization might include civil rights law or First Amendment issues such as free speech, etc. The field, clearly is vast, and the opportunities for individual emphasis almost endless.

Aside from the above emphasis on the domestic side of the operations of the American political system, there is also the opportunity to focus on the foreign or international side of American government with the area of specialization of American foreign policy and diplomacy. This area, too, has a variety of subspecializations and is a tremendous preparation for those seeking careers in foreign or diplomatic service either through the State Department, by taking the Foreign Service examination or through any of the intelligence related agencies or through service in the armed forces and the Pentagon.

These, then, are the various areas of emphasis dealing with the subfield of American government in political science. Political science, however, has many other subfields as well, which we will briefly mention here for those interested in pursuing those options at some point in their student careers.

Political science in addition to American government, constitutional law, public administration and public policy, also emphasizes international relations, comparative politics, political theory, international political economy, and now a new interdisciplinary field of studies, international or global studies.

With the exception of political theory or political philosophy as it is sometimes called, the other subfields mentioned here all have an "international" emphasis. By that we mean to say that their emphasis is directed away from a domestic look at American politics, and that though they may include

America prominently in their discussions, do not emphasize America primarily as their focus of study.

Political theory is unique among the subfields of political science in that its emphasis is neither "domestic" nor "international" per se, it is foundational. Political theory studies the various thinkers, ideas and ideologies that underlie the very fabric of the study of politics and give it its language and vocabulary. We speak of Republicans and Democrats in American politics, but where do the ideas and concepts come from that Republicans and Democrats call their own? We speak of "popular sovereignty" and "consent of the governed" in democratic political systems, but where do these ideas come from? This and more is the subject matter of political theory or political philosophy.

Comparative politics is an area of study that makes use of similar themes to those studied in a course on American government, only it expands its scope of study to many more political systems than just one, and compares them with a view to gaining greater insight into the workings of each, as well as gaining greater certainty as to which political system is superior to others. Comparative politics divides itself into conceptual study and case study emphases, and then within the case study emphasis, divides itself up by region and even further by country. It is therefore possible to find individuals in the subfield of comparative politics that have specialized on, say, Western Europe as a region and then have further specialized on one country in this region, say, France, and then have specialized on one or several aspects of the French political system such as its presidency, or its legislature or its political parties, etc. These kinds of specializations are particularly useful to individuals seeking to enter into the U.S. Foreign Service or seeking to serve as area experts in the U.S. State Department or the equivalent of both of these in other countries.

International relations, international political economy and the new field of international or global studies are all areas of emphasis related to each other in that they originally sprung from or are offshoots of international relations. Indeed, comparative politics, too, can be considered an offshoot of international relations, as it emerged as a result of the perceived shortcomings in international relations in the 1950s and 1960s through the efforts of mostly American scholars.

International relations deals with the area of foreign policy, diplomacy, and war. The subject matter of international relations, in fact, is the study of what makes for conflict or war in the international system and what makes for peace. There are various schools of thought in this subfield of political science, emphasizing one or the other aspect of international politics, and, as with other subfields, there are also a great number of areas of specialization in this subfield, such as arms race and disarmament issues, international law and diplomacy, international organizations, etc. Specialization in this subfield is ideal for individuals seeking careers in national and international diplomacy or careers such as national security advisor to the president or the like.

International political economy is a relatively new subfield of political science that emerged as a result of the need to pay heed to economic forces and their interaction with political dynamics in the international arena. International political economy emphasizes the role of politics and political institutions in arenas traditionally considered part of the economic field such as international trade. It is a move away from a purely political science approach to the international arena as well as a move away from a purely economic approach to the arena of relations between nations. Individuals seeking careers in international business or law as well as foreign service or international diplomacy in institutions such as the United Nations or the OECD, the World Bank or the International Monetary Fund, are well advised to study this subfield of political science.

Last but not least, the field of international or global studies, the newest arrival on the scene, tries to bring together more than two disciplines and tries to look at the global phenomena we face through a multidisciplinary lens. Areas of study in this field are globalization and its effects, the environment, trade, diseases, etc., all phenomena that go beyond the boundaries and borders of any one nation or political system and that require international or global responses for their solution. Individuals studying this field will not only apply their skills in the traditional arenas of international relations but also beyond that in new and evolving international bodies that increasingly take such transdisciplinary approaches, such as the United Nations, the World Trade Organization, or the like.

Generally, careers for individuals majoring in political science or any one of its subfields include becoming public servants at one level or another, from local government employees to state and national government levels. It also includes, of course seeking public office at the local, state or national level. Many political scientists also go into the field of law and combine their knowledge of politics with that of law to become lawyers or prosecutors or district attorneys and judges at all levels of government. Expertise in political science can also lead to careers as political advisors and political consultants at various levels of government or in the private sector with interest groups, the media or domestic and foreign firms.

Emphasis in political science can also lead to a career in the foreign service or in international diplomacy as already stated. Finally, last but not least, it can lead to a teaching career to train future political scientists who would then occupy any one of the above listed positions.

Now that we have covered the lay of the land regarding the various areas of emphasis and the eventual outlets for these areas of emphasis in political science, let us focus on the subject at hand, the study of how America is governed. We will start by defining our terms.

 # **Definitions**

Before we begin, we need to define the basic terms encountered in this course. We will start with the most obvious ones.

What is political science? How is it different from politics?

The simplest way to look at these two questions is to imagine the following situation: As students, we, at some point need to study biology as part of our general education (GE) requirements. Biology is the study or science of life (the "*logos* of *bios*"). In biology, we study life, and more generally, the laws of nature, of evolution. We study species and subspecies; learn about their anatomies, biospheres, and ecosystems; about what makes a cell split and reproduce. We learn about the immutable principles that guide observable life and thus learn what constitutes life.

Now, as we all know, we—students, teachers, human beings in general—are part of that life. We are alive and, thus, the subject matter of biology. In being alive we also know something about life and what keeps us and other living things alive, not as a matter of scientific knowledge necessarily, but as a matter of experience.

Putting all these elements together we can say the following: As living beings we have experience of, and experience life by living it. As a result, we know a thing or two about life and living. But the sheer fact of living and having experience of it is not sufficient for us to be able to fathom the laws that underlie life; that are its guiding principles. Being alive is not a sufficient condition for us to be able to understand the principles guiding life. For that we need a science of life, biology, to explain those principles to us.

We do not argue that we are experts in the science of life because we happen to have lived for a while and thus know what we are talking about. We understand that living and understanding the underlying principles guiding life are two very different things. Thus we do not expect to be exempt from our biology GE requirement by producing a birth certificate and a driver license.

So it is also with political science and politics. Politics, to paraphrase one of the founding fathers of the discipline, the Greek philosopher Aristotle (who, incidentally, was also the founding father of biology), is what individuals do when living in concert with others in a community. In other words, politics is the stuff of our daily interactions in the public arena.

It involves not only our doings but also those of others and our observation of their doings. It also involves our observations or opinions about them and us. Just as we "do" what biology studies by living daily, we also "do" politics by being in (to use the Greek word) the *polis*, the city, the political community. And we all live in one political community or another called our country. No one lives outside the political community. But it is still one thing to be in a political community, even to participate in its public life in a major way, say, as a politician, and quite another to know as a matter of scientific observation and theoretical formulation what are the underlying principles of politics and the political community.

Just as we need biology to tell us about the fundamental principles of physical life, so we need political science to tell us about the fundamental principles of political life. We cannot claim knowledge of political science by arguing that we have lived in a political community for a while and thus have opinions about politics, just as we cannot claim knowledge of biology by arguing that we have lived and thus have knowledge of life. And, yes, we cannot claim exemption to the American institutions requirement of "American government" in American colleges by producing proof of residency or showing knowledge of the latest issue on the front page of the *Los Angeles Times*, or by having "opinions" about politics. Political science does not deal with these subject matters but rather with those that underlie them. It teaches us about the principles that guide the political system of which we are a part, and it tells us what the laws are that make it "tick." It also tells us *why* we have political opinions, as opposed to observing *that* we have them.

So, to make a long story short, political science is the science of politics in the same way biology is the science of *bios*, of life. Both are a larger reflection on the underlying causes and laws of their subject matter and thus not to be confused with their subject matter. And, yes, both are complicated, though it could be argued for anyone who has survived their biology requirement that biology may be harder than political science, though the jury may still be out on that.

What is the political system and how is this different from the government?

Each discipline has its own language and each discipline tries to be very rigorous in its use of language and in its distinctions. Scientific language is very precise and precision helps understanding by clearing up confusion. Thus each element that is the subject matter of a discipline is described as precisely as possible and strictly distinguished from other elements within the subject so as to achieve maximum clarity. This is true of biology; it is also true of political science.

Now, the most obvious subject of study for political science is government. Government both in the sense of the governing institution (e.g., the government of the United States or the government of Canada or of France) and government as the act of governing, that is, the act of running the day-to-day affairs of a country so that what is being decided by those in power and with power actually gets carried out and bears results.

This distinction between government as an institution and government as the act of governing is not always clarified in textbooks. In fact, it is cause for much confusion. Take your textbook, for example. It probably has the phrase "American government" somewhere in its title. The title of this course certainly does. But both the course and the textbook are about more than simply "the American government," strictly speaking. In other words, they are about more than the three branches that make up government: the legislative, the executive, and the judicial branches. Both your textbooks and these classes are also about government as the act of governing, and thus the textbooks and the syllabi contain more than simply three chapters and three lectures, respectively.

A quick glance at the table of contents of your textbooks will reveal that, aside from the introductory chapters on definitions and historical background and the founding documents of the country, your books also include chapters on the relationship between the national government and the governments of the states (usually under the rubric of federalism). It also includes chapters on the relationship between people and their government (usually discussed under civil rights and civil liberties); a chapter on interest groups, one on political parties, three on each of the branches of government proper, one at least on the bureaucracy, one on the media, and then perhaps additional ones on policymaking, etc.

All this is about more than the three branches of government. This is about how a country, in this case the United States, is governed and what elements enter into the equation to make the act of governing possible. This entire process needs to be given a different name to distinguish it from the stricter meaning of the term "government," which refers to the three branches named above. This larger edifice composed of many interacting institutions that make governing a country possible is called the political system. It includes the three branches of government, the legislative, the executive, and the judiciary, prominently within it, but is much larger than just these three. It is this notion of the political system and, more specifically, the American political system that we are going to be considering in this course. A study of the political system and its interaction with the people of this country is what a study of government in America is about.

What is the subject matter of politics and what does political science study?

Earlier, we said that politics is the stuff of our daily interactions in the public arena, and that political science teaches us about the principles that guide the political system of which we are a part, and that it tells us what the laws are that make this political system "tick." But, if we were to ask point-blank what is politics about and what does political science study, the answer would have to be one word: power. Politics is about power and political science is the study of power in all its manifestations in the political arena. Some famous definitions of politics can also be taken as definitions of power and show how interrelated these two terms are. Harold Laswell defines politics as "who gets what, when and how." That can also apply to power. If one has power, one decides "who gets what, when and how!" David Easton, another prominent political scientist defined politics as the "authoritative allocation of values." Power itself was one of those values, but aside from that, to authoritatively allocate anything one must have power, thus power is the means one seeks to attain in order to then be able to *authoritatively* allocate values to others. The two terms, "politics" and "power," are intricately linked, and modern political science is the study of what power consists of in the political arena, how it is applied, to what ends and by what means, how it is gained, how it lost, how it is misapplied, etc.

The American political scientist Robert Dahl defined power as: A's ability to make B do something that B would otherwise not do on its own. In other words, power is a device by which one achieves ones own goals despite obstacles and resistance by others. Often, power is considered a scarce resource, and the power game considered one of zero sums where my gains equal your losses. Though that need not always be the case, the game of politics often presents itself that way. Two candidates for presidential office, for instance, cannot *both* win. One must lose, and thus the gains of one are equal to the losses of the other. But not all political situations are like that; often politics (i.e., the game of power) is also called the art of compromise and the art of the possible, in order to emphasize that in many situations win-win scenarios are worked out. Politics is also about give and take, but it is much more appealing to think of it as a wipeout game, and people often perceive it that way.

We have talked about the notion of games and about the give and take that goes along with the game of politics. When we talk of games we must also talk of rules of the game. The game of politics is played with a variety of rules depending on the context in which it is played or, to put it differently, depending on the political framework within which it is played. Now, there are a variety of frameworks within which the game of politics can be played but there is only one that has come to be acceptable to the people of the United States. That framework is the democratic one.

What is democracy? It is a specific kind of game rule, very different from other game rules, and very reminiscent of Robert Fulghum's oft-quoted rules from his book *All I Really Need to Know I Learned in Kindergarten*. It's about taking turns, about acknowledging and living with political loss, but also about getting to try again. It is not about punching others in the face but rather about arguing one's own point to the best of one's ability and letting others be the judge of the merit of one's argument. It is about playing the game of politics in a civil and civilized manner, with one overriding concern, that the power and rights of the people always be considered paramount. The democratic rules involve such key concepts as popular sovereignty, legitimacy based on the notion of the consent of the governed, a constitution as the overriding law of the land, regular elections, equality before the law, inalienable rights for the people, protections for the people from the powers that be, rights the people can over time demand and get from the powers that be, etc. Democracy is about fairness. It is the first type of game rule that considers the wellbeing of the mass of players as more important than that of the few and more powerful ones.

So, putting these points together, let us see what it is we are dealing with in this course. We are dealing with a political study of the way America is governed. Saying this means saying that we are looking with a political science lens at the political dynamic of the American political system, with a view to ultimately understand how power in America is brought to bear on the political system to achieve the goals of the various players involved.

MORE DEFINITIONS

When studying American government one also needs to focus on what is unique about the American political system, on what distinguishes the American political system from other systems similar to it.

The key phrase that encapsulates that which is peculiarly American about the American political system is the phrase "American political culture." What do we mean by that term? Textbooks define political culture as a set of shared values or the sum of attitudes of a people toward their system of government. It is therefore clear that political cultures differ from country to country, but that there are some common themes found in political systems. In other words, all democratic political systems share certain characteristics and emphasize similar values. The citizens of each of these different political systems give these values slightly different emphases depending on how they came to hold them in the first place; i.e., what trials and tribulations they had to endure to achieve what they have today, what challenges they had to face.

Everyone agrees that the key components of American political culture are the notions of liberty or freedom, equality, and democracy. In other words, these concepts are the core ideas that all Americans share, and they define with a peculiar American twist what distinguishes them from the way the French or the Germans might define these terms.

Americans did not invent any of these ideas. They are much older than most countries in the world today. Democracy is as old as human communities. Longing for freedom, arguably, is equally as old. Ancient Athens was one of the first political systems to experiment with democracy in a spectacular way. It is still the model for what democracy really stands for, the rule of and by the people. Freedom and equality were concepts debated not only in Athens but also in seventeenth-century England and eighteenth-century France. In fact, a group of philosophers called the "social contract theorists," first became famous for espousing these ideas and formulating them in their writings. One of them particularly, John Locke, became the inspiration for the philosopher of the American Revolution, Thomas Jefferson. It was Jefferson who first eloquently formulated the ideals of the future republic, but he would have been the first to admit that he was only continuing what others like Locke and Thomas Paine had begun before him.

Jefferson formulated the vocabulary of American political culture in the Declaration of Independence. The first two paragraphs of the Declaration spell out what America has meant politically ever since: the right of rebellion against unjust government, the notion of equality, the notion of unalienable rights, the notion of just government as being government by consent of the governed. In other words, the concepts of freedom, equality, and democracy. (For excerpts of the Declaration of Independence, see Appendix B.)

Democracy has already been defined above. Let us just add here that democracy in America did not mean direct democracy on the Athenian model but rather representative democracy, and, as such, a republic more on the Roman model. To paraphrase the Gettysburg Address, American democracy is not so much about government *by the people* as it is about government *for the people* through their representatives. (For text of Gettysburg Address, see Appendix H.)

Liberty or freedom should be defined next. Jefferson wrote in the Declaration of Independence that all human beings were endowed with certain unalienable rights, and that among these were "life, liberty, and the pursuit of happiness." Thus, the concept of freedom is intimately associated with the notion of rights in the American context. Rights imply abilities on the part of the people to engage in certain courses of action without the worry that they will be limited in them arbitrarily. It also implies guarantees to the people, by government, that government will not apply its power to limit people's freedom to engage in these actions. Thus, freedom has two aspects to it in this context: the freedom to do certain things and the freedom from government doing certain things to the people. We derive this discussion and distinction partly from the work of Sir Isaiah Berlin, from his famous inaugural lecture at the University of Oxford in 1958 titled "Two Concepts of Liberty." The notion of "freedom to" is called positive freedom. The notion of "freedom from," which Isaiah Berlin championed, is called negative freedom (negative not in the sense of "bad" but rather in the sense of a "thou shalt not" directed to government). This is the meaning of the first words of the First Amendment of the U.S. Constitution, "Congress shall make no law. . ." Another version of "freedom from" was given in President Roosevelt's famous Four Freedoms speech, where he listed the things individuals everywhere should be "free from": Free from fear, from want, but also "free to" speak and "free to" worship their God in their own way. (For the text of President Roosevelt's Address to Congress in 1941, see Appendix K.)

Equality is the last of the trio of core American political values. Americans have always been ambivalent about this notion of equality, from the first time it was mentioned in American political documents (such as the Declaration of Independence), to today, where it is discussed more in terms of its connection with liberty than with the stricter notion of equality, which, when viewed this way, is understood to have more economic and social implications.

Equality has two meanings in the American context. One is the notion of "political equality," which reflects both Jefferson's notion of "all men" being "created equal," and his notion of legitimate government being government by "consent of the governed." Political equality means "one man, one vote." It implies that in a democracy, when it comes to exercising one's power to choose one's representatives, or when it comes to the representatives legislating in the legislative chambers, no one's voice counts for more than anyone else's and thus all are equal in power in that respect. The other meaning of equality in the American context is that of "equality of opportunity." Equality of opportunity here means everyone having the same chance at success, without the worry of obstacles in their way. This is what is implied in the notion of the American Dream. It is also this meaning of equality that is present in America's emphasis on, and preference for, free-market policies. The injunction of "absence of obstacles" is an injunction to government to step out of the way or, alternately, to remove societal obstacles so that people have an equal chance. This notion of equality was championed by the late Nobel laureate and free-market economist Milton Friedman and popularized in his book and film series *Free to Choose* (1980). Both these notions of equality are intricately linked with the idea of fairness in the American political psyche.

If we were to add one more concept here that would round out American political culture, it would be that of separation of church and state. The idea is enshrined in the First Amendment of the U.S. Constitution, in both the Establishment and Free Exercise clauses of that amendment, and also in this clause of Article VI of the U.S. Constitution: "No religious test shall ever be required as a qualification to any office or public trust under the United States." The notion of freedom of religion and its concomitant notion of separation of church and state derive from, among other things, the founding history of this country. When the Pilgrims arrived in New England, they were fleeing religious persecution and seeking the right to practice their religion freely. Though they later became quite intolerant of dissent in their own ranks, this idea of founding a society in which individuals could be free from the threat of persecution for their religious beliefs, and free from a government that would enforce an official religion, remains to this day a cornerstone of the American political culture. This is true despite the rise of the influence of religious groups in politics and the many instances of the presence of religion in politics such as the phrase "So help me God" at the end of the oath of office of the president of the United States (a phrase that does not exist in the language of the Constitution in Article II, section 1), or in the moments of silence or prayer that open and close sessions of the houses Congress (there are even official chaplains for these institutions).

Now that we have taken some time to explore some of the fundamental concepts we are dealing with in this course, let us proceed to an analysis of the major themes of the course. (For a full list of the themes, see Outline of Themes.)

Part I: Theory

CHAPTER 1

Democracy

Democracy is discussed generally as both a form of government and an idea or ideal of governance. When discussed as a form of government, democracy is divided into two categories: direct and indirect or representative democracy (see chart below). Little needs to be said today about direct democracy because it no longer exists as a form of government. True, there are "pockets" of direct democratic decision-making, such as the New England town meetings and the Swiss cantonal and municipal meetings, but these local modes of decision-making are each in turn subject to a larger governmental arrangement—that of representative democracy—and thus cannot be considered forms of government in and of themselves anymore.

Direct democracy did exist, however, and it left an indelible mark on our political imagination. I am referring, of course, to the brief but glorious example of Athenian democracy during the fifth century BCE, even though Athens was a mixed form of democracy, partly direct and partly representative. This form of government was described by one of the most formidable statesmen of the time, Pericles:

> Our constitution is called a democracy because power is in the hands not of a minority but of the whole of the people. When it is a question of settling private disputes, everyone is equal before the law; when it is a question of putting one person before another in positions of public responsibility, what counts is not membership of a particular class, but the actual ability which the man possesses. No one, so long as he has it in him to be of service to the state, is kept in political obscurity because of poverty. (Thucydides, II, 37)

Aristotle further describes this form of government as one where citizens were able to both "rule and be ruled" (Aristotle, *Politics*, III, 4).

From our vantage point, however, this form of government was far from perfect in that it was based on two institutions that are odious to our political and moral sensibilities today: slavery and limited suffrage. Slaves were the engines of the political and economic machinery of Athens as of all other cities of antiquity. Slaves were the prisoners of war who were put to work in the victor's seat of power. The condition of slavery devolved on one's progeny unless one was freed by one's master or freed by one's kin through victory in battle. Limited suffrage and thus full political participation was reserved for male citizens. In Athens that meant every male born in Athens regardless of status (excluding slaves).

Despite these two shortcomings, the principles enunciated in Pericles' oration were worthy of admiration and, today, they represent the ideals that democracy and democratic forms of government strive to achieve: universal suffrage, political equality, equal participation in the decision-making process, responsible government, accountability, and popular sovereignty. These are the standards against which we measure our existing forms of government and it is for this reason that we call this form of democratic government "ideal."

Representative, or indirect, democracy is the form of democracy that exists today. Its origin goes back to the Roman republic. In fact, the term "republic" is synonymous with representative democracy for this very reason. The Roman republic, which ended with the assassination of Julius Caesar and the rise of the Roman Empire, combined in itself many of the present-day elements of representative government: elections, legislative bodies making laws in the name of the people, balanced representation of all segments of the citizenry, and equality before the law. However, modern representative democracies derive more from the British, American, and French revolutions of the seventeenth and eighteenth centuries than they do from the Roman experience, even though they borrowed from Rome far more than just the names of its institutions. Still, the American experiment must stand out as the blueprint for most, if not all, modern democracies. A careful study of the American form of representative democracy gives us a valuable insight into the make-up and the possible variations in types of representative democracies around the world today.

Customarily, when we discuss modern representative democracy as a form of government, we divide our discussion into a variety of categories. With each variation, and the combination of that variation with others from the list below, we find operating a different kind of representative democracy. What that means in practice is that we find different patterns of interaction between the people and their representatives; we find different distributions of power; we find different internal dynamics in legislatures and between legislatures and executives, such that as a result we find different kinds of governance all together, even though they all fall under the category of representative democracy.

As any American citizen who is aware of Western European political systems knows, political life in England or France is very different from that of the United States and the difference is not due to use of different languages but rather to the existence of different arrangements within those political systems. These different possible arrangements are what the chart below is about. It aims to be exhaustive, but the astute observer may still find one or more additional and subtler categories that enable us to further distinguish between one and the other form of representative democracy.

Direct	Indirect/
(Ideal)	**Representative**

Republic

Constitutional Monarchy

Types of Representative Democracies

Presidential   Parliamentary

Hybrid

Types of Executive/Legislative

Relations in Republics

Unanimity/Majority/Plurality

Single Member District/Proportional Repres.

Electoral Systems

Unicameral   Bicameral

Symmetrical/Asymmetrical

Type of Legislature

Two-Party   Multi-Party

Party Systems

Party Discipline   No Party Discipline

Party Structure in Legislatures

Unitary

Confederate

Federal

Territorial Divisions in Democracies

Pluralist   Majoritarian

Hyperpluralist/Elitist

Models of Democratic Politics

Any discussion of democracy, not as a form of government but as an idea and a concept, falls under the rubric "democratic theory" or "views" on democracy. When discussed in this context, one looks at the notion of democracy by focusing on the substance or essence of the term itself or by focussing on the minimal procedural requirements by which democracy is achieved in practice. These two views of democracy are called the substantive and procedural views, respectively. The best explanation of the meaning of these terms and the best scholarly exchange on the matter is the exchange between Sydney Hook and Howard Zinn. Howard Zinn espouses the "substantive view" of democracy and Sydney Hook defends the "procedural view" of democracy. As is evident from the reading, Hook's position is the conservative position, whereas Zinn's view is the liberal one. (See Appendix L for the Hook-Zinn exchange.)

Another distinction made about democracy is the notion of the pattern of interaction between the people and their political system. How people interact with their political system determines what the tenor and "flavor" of that democracy will be. Generally, when looking at it from this point of view, democracy is described as either majoritarian or pluralist. Let us turn to this discussion next in Chapter 2, "Models of Democracy."

Models of Democracy

There are various ways to describe how democracy presents itself to us, or what kind of democracy we are dealing with when looking at a democratic political system. Not all democratic political systems are the same simply because they are democratic of the representative kind. They differ in how the interaction between the people and the political system is structured in that particular context. In some democratic political systems, the people as citizens play a major and on-going role in the day-to-day politics of that system; in others the people are mostly absent from day-to-day politics, instead interest groups become the intermediary between the people and the political system for their day-to-day politics. These differing modes of interaction between the people and their political systems make for very different kinds of systems, and thus it is important to classify them differently and understand what the basis for distinction is.

In the literature, two concepts are used to distinguish two different types of representative democratic political systems: majoritarian and pluralist. Majoritarianism, in this context, implies that large numbers of people interact with their political system in an attempt to influence outcomes as individuals (i.e., not as members of organized groups). Examples of majoritarianism (i.e., of situations where the relationship between the people and their political system is as defined above) are voting, participating in demonstrations, letter-writing campaigns, sit-ins, rallies, and the like, in order to influence members of the political system. Now, all democratic political systems exhibit some of these modes of participation at one point or another. All democratic political systems certainly have their people participate in voting, which is the universal means by which people bestow legitimacy on their political systems in democracies. But not all democracies exhibit this type of interaction between the people and the political system as a rule. Those that do—that is, those democracies where the people, as a rule, interact with their system through the above means to get their way—are described as majoritarian in flavor, so to speak.

Since not all democratic political systems are structured such that people interact with them as a rule in the above described manner, we must also have a term to describe democratic systems where the people interact with the political system to influence outcomes, not as individuals, but as members of organized groups. That term is "pluralism." Viewed this way, pluralism implies that large numbers of people interact with their political system in an attempt to influence outcomes as members of organized groups (i.e., not as individuals). Examples of pluralism, thus defined, are interest groups vying for access to members of the political system to get outcomes that favor the members of those groups. It is for this reason that this type of pluralism has also been termed "interest-group pluralism."

Now there are certain normative assumptions behind each of these two models of democracy that need to be explained briefly. Majoritarianism lays claim to being the essence of democracy. It holds that democracy implies the express and expressed will of the people (a majority thereof at the very least), and what greater proof of the expressed will of the people than large numbers of people speaking their mind to power individually in order to achieve the outcomes they desire? Pluralism, on the other hand, lays claim to being what democracy truly implies because it holds that democracy implies the free expression and competition of ideas with the result of the best idea winning, and what greater proof of that than interest groups competing for the attention of the political system and the best ones winning the day and getting their way?

Both approaches, of course, speak to the heart of the democratic matter, and in the end, there is no hard and fast way of deciding which of the two approaches is the more democratic one. They both are, and it depends on the political culture of the countries in which democracy has flourished as to which mode will dominate.

The American democracy has tended to favor pluralism, as defined above, as the dominant mode by which people interact with their political system. There are a variety of reasons for this, not the least of which is an historical distrust of mass popular movements of any kind, evidenced by the reaction of the Founding Fathers to such popular uprisings as Shays' Rebellion, and carried all the way through to the reaction of the political system to the more recent demonstrations by the people in Seattle and in Washington, D.C., against the World Trade Organization and the International Monetary Fund and World Bank, respectively.

Preference for pluralism also derives from the fact that pluralism as a model of politics describes a situation very reminiscent of the preferred mode of economic interaction in the United States as well, that of free-market capitalism. The model of the free market is one of roughly equal sized competitors with roughly equal information and roughly equal access, competing for gains (profit). At the end of the day, the idea is that there will be some winners and some losers, but that the losers will have had a fair chance *and* that the next day, today's losers could be that day's winners. In other words, nothing predetermines the outcome other than personal initiative and perhaps a little luck. There are no permanent winners or losers. The result of that interaction structured in this way is *fairness,* the very cornerstone of the entire edifice of the free market. Pluralism in the political realm has the same overtones and implications in people's minds, and thus has a similar following. And so long as the system in fact operates along those lines, there is little argument that this constitutes a fair kind of system. But the day-to-day reality of politics is often very far from this rather idyllic and innocent picture. In reality, pluralism often exists only in name and not in fact.

A truer picture of the reality of interaction of people with the American political system would be one described by Robert Lineberry as *hyperpluralism.* Hyperpluralism, literally means "too much pluralism," and taken literally, therefore, makes little sense. What the term means to describe is too much interest group influence on the system, presumably to the exclusion of other interests, namely those of the people who are not organized as groups. Another way, however, of looking at the notion of hyperpluralism is to look at it as a term describing a situation where *some* interest groups, namely, the larger ones, have managed to rig the system in such a manner that they get their way *most* of the time, to the exclusion of smaller groups and the people who are not organized in groups at all. Theodore Lowi coined the term "interest-group liberalism" to describe the influence wielded by these groups and the attention paid to them by the lawmakers to the detriment of other interests in society. Viewed this way, hyperpluralism is not just another version of pluralism, but rather an aberration thereof, and, in as much as it more accurately describes the nature and reality of the interaction of people with the political system of the United States, a matter of grave concern. This situation has led Lowi, Ginsberg, and Weir, the authors of the text *We the People,* to call the American political system a "quasi-democracy."

Still farther away from the notion of pluralism is the notion of elitism. Elitism refers to the successful capturing of political influence over the political system by *one* group alone, to the *exclusion* of all others. Usually, that group is identified as "the rich" in this political system, but that would imply that the rich are, in fact, in accord as to all their political demands and act in unison to achieve them. Since this is a very hard case to make, elitism best refers to systems like those of Europe before the democratic revolutions, or of South Africa under apartheid or the antebellum U.S., or the south until the 1960s and early 1970s. It would be a stretch to describe the United States today as an elitist political system, despite the fact that the rich do indeed have sizable influence on political outcomes in the United States.

Another way, still, to look at this discussion is to see to whom the political system tends to respond. If the political system tends to respond to the will of the majority of the people, then one can call that a majoritarian democracy. If not, then pluralist or perhaps even hyperpluralist. This is how Janda, Berry, and

Goldman address the question in the reading entitled "Does Government Do What People Want?" (See Appendix M for excerpt by Kenneth Janda et al..)

Having looked at the concepts underlying the notion of democracy it is now well to turn our attention to the way democracies organize themselves institutionally and territorially for us to be able to get a better understanding of how the government of the United States functions and why it exhibits the institutional arrangements it does.

CHAPTER 3

The Model of the Political System

From a discussion of the models of Democracy, we move on to a study of the political system. This discussion is a general discussion of any political system, with no specific reference to the American one, but the astute student will realize that it is particularly applicable to the American political system and thus its relevance here.

One of the terms that we discussed originally was the term "political system." We distinguished it from the term government and elaborated on the difference. To recapitulate briefly, the distinction has to do with the fact that government is one of the many institutions within the political system, but that the political system is larger than that and includes political parties, interest groups, and the bureaucracy as part of itself. Together, these institutions enable the system to produce policies, the result of which is the ability to govern a people in a territory. Political systems can be defined as a coherent set of institutions working together toward a given outcome.

The model we use in these lectures to describe the American political system and the way it functions, is derived from the model used by Almond and Powell in their book *Comparative Politics* (2003). It is the best descriptive model of any when it comes to explaining how and why this system in particular, the American system, operates the way it does. This has to do with the fact that the American political system is a pluralist system, as discussed earlier, and that the model proposed here accommodates that fact best in the way it emphasizes the role of interest groups in the political system. But more on that later. Let us turn to a discussion of the model for now.

Political systems are collections of institutions working together to make the task of governance possible. They do not exist in a vacuum. They are at the center of, and operate within a larger context referred to as the domestic environment. The domestic environment is the territory and the people, the society, over which that political system governs. The domestic environment and the political system together make up the political entity called a country, in this case the United States. (See modified Almond and Powell Model of the Political System in Appendix A.)

The political system is a complex set of institutions working together. It is complex not only in terms of the many institutions working together but also in terms of the functions that both the system and these institutions perform in order to make governance possible. Each institution within the political system contributes to and facilitates the task of governing, and the system as a whole also helps set the stage so that governing becomes and is possible. When the system itself carries out functions to facilitate the act of governing, those functions are called "system" functions. When the institutions within the political system carry out functions to make governance possible those functions are called "process" functions.

System functions are those actions taken by the system to facilitate the act of governing and simultaneously preserving the political system intact, with minimal change over time. These tasks are performed with the idea of achieving stability and order and to ensure the survival of the system. No political system strives to see itself extinguished. All political systems inherently and automatically seek to ensure their own survival. In a sense, this is also what "governing" means. Why this meaning of the term is not offensive in the American context has to do with the fact that in this political system people are equal stakeholders in the survival of the system. They are, in a sense, its creators and sustainers, whereas in nondemocratic systems the people are not only not considered equal players, they are often also seen as potential threats to the survival of the system and thus kept under tight control.

There are three system functions performed by the political system: socialization, recruitment, and communication. Socialization is the largest and most complex of these three functions and will be discussed separately in the lecture on socialization, political opinion, and participation in chapter 8. Recruitment refers to the act of bringing those into the system who will most ideally fit the task of continuing the system on its even keel. Recruitment is a necessary and essential function in that outgoing members of the system need to be replaced with new ones in order to maintain the systems ability to govern. Recruitment is also related to the function of communication. Communication refers to the ability of the system to tell the people in the domestic environment what is expected of them and to its ability, in turn, to hear from them what they expect of it. Communication and recruitment both are related to the function of socialization as well, in that communication is a critical means by which socialization takes place, and recruitment really is the end result of the successful socialization process, for what else is the aim of political socialization other than bringing forth the kind of individual who would sustain the system best.

There is an interesting point to be made at this junction about this notion of the "political system" and its carrying out of functions. The political system, as such, is an abstraction. It does not exist as a tangible object in the same way as the executive branch exists, or the Congress, or this or that political party, etc. A political system "exists" only in the aggregate of the institutions that constitute it, and is visible or tangible only in the product it generates: policies. Thus, to speak of the political system performing functions is really to say that the institutions within it performs those tasks or functions on behalf of that political system, while simultaneously performing the tasks or functions that they perform as a result of the kind of institution they are. For instance, the task of recruitment is not performed by a separate office in the political system called "system recruiting office." That task is performed on behalf of the system by the many institutions within it as part of carrying out their other functions as well. Interest groups, political parties, the three branches of government, and the bureaucracy all recruit into the political system new faces and new blood, as part of and in addition to what they do, day in day out inside the system. For this reason, I call "primary" functions, those functions that the institutions perform within the political system as part of what they are, and those functions they perform on behalf of the system, I call "secondary" and/or "tertiary" functions, as the case may be. In other words, what is the primary function of an interest group within the political system? Presumably, it is to bring issues to the attention of the system by organizing itself in such a manner that when it presents its views to the system the system can hear them and react positively to that request. But what does an interest group also do within the system? Well, for one thing it brings new people in and familiarizes them with the political process, which is a complex one. For another, it might provide those people with a platform from which to launch a more elaborate career within the political system as advocates, members of political parties, and perhaps even candidates themselves, etc. In so many words, the interest group also recruits for the system as part of what it does naturally, namely put issues before the system and advocate for those issues.

This is a good transition to the notion of process functions. Almond and Powell use the term "process function" to describe the functions the institutions within the system perform to enable the flow of policy, from input of an issue into the system to output by the system of a policy, to occur. (Please see modified Almond and Powell model in Appendix A.) There seems to be a natural sequence of functions, occurring within the system, from the time an issue enters the system to the time it exits it as a policy. That sequence would put interest groups and their function first, followed by political parties and the task(s) they perform within the political system, followed by the very complex series of tasks that the three branches of government perform in sequence, followed, lastly by the task the bureaucracy performs, culminating in the implementation of a policy in the domestic environment. Once a policy is implemented, the people have a chance to react to it in a variety of ways, and, to, in due time, turn those reactions into new inputs into the system and thus close the loop referred to as feedback loop.

The primary function of interest groups, in the context of Almond and Powell's model, is to articulate issues. Articulation refers to the ability of interest groups to clarify and amplify an issue for the system to be able to hear it and process it. In an interest group pluralist system like that of the United States, the role of interest groups as links between the people and the system becomes almost paramount.

Next is the role or function of political parties. According to the model, their main function is that of aggregation. Aggregation refers to the ability of political parties to gather up the variously articulated issues into a coherent whole that will form the essence of their platform. The platforms of the political parties are the collected themes which the political parties want to see turned into policy. They are the expression of the ideology of the respective parties.

This, however, is not the only role of political parties within the political system. In addition to appreciating issues articulated by interest groups into platforms, political parties also recruit and support candidates for office. This is one of the most visible roles of the parties and it will be discussed further in depth on parties and interest groups (Chapter 10).

The role of government is that of policy formulation or policy making. The legislative and executive branches work together in this process. In the United States, the president proposes initiatives he would like to see become policy. With the exception of the president's power of issuing executive orders and thus turning his expressed will into policy directly, Congress must go along with the president's proposals in all other cases by legislating to that effect. The cooperation between these two branches results in policy making or formulation. Only in extraordinary cases does the judicial branch play a role in this process, and then only if there is a challenge to the expressed will of either or both of the other two branches.

Lastly, the role or function of the bureaucracy. The bureaucracy is, in a sense, the extension of the executive branch. The bureaucracy's primary role is to therefore carry out or implement the will of the executive, and more generally that of government as a whole. It is through the bureaucracy that the policies of the government are put into action and implemented upon society and the people that reside in it. The bureaucracy is anything from the Forest Service to the Secret Service and the many agencies and bureaus in between. Once the bureaucracy has implemented a policy, the people react to it either positively or neutrally or negatively. If the reaction is neutral or positive, the feedback to the system will be one of support for the policy and thus one encouraging continuation of that course of action. If the reaction is negative and of sufficient strength, then the system's reaction will be one of changing the policy in all likelihood. This process is described by the feedback loop. (See Almond & Powell model in Appendix A).

This, in a very general way, concludes our discussion of the model of the political system. The points made here will be applied to each of the individual discussions dealing with the various elements or institutions within the political system. These points will also be applied to the notions of socialization, opinion building and participation, which will be discussed in Chapter 8.

CHAPTER 4

Parliamentary, Presidential and Hybrid Forms of Government

Democratic governments can be differentiated by focusing on how they organize themselves with regard to the relationship between their executive and legislative branches. This different way of organizing is discussed and defined in textbooks as the difference between parliamentary and presidential forms of government. This is relevant to the study of the government of the United States because the presidential form of government, which is a hallmark of the American government, was an American invention, as was the territorial division of federalism, which we will be discussing in the next section.

The book definition of the parliamentary form of government is that of a system that *fuses* the executive and legislative branches. The presidential form is defined as one that *strictly separates* the legislative and executive branches. Before we go on, however, a note on the terminology. The parliamentary form of government is termed "parliamentary" because it derives its essential shape from the decisions the legislature or parliament takes. It is also called "parliamentary" because it is the form of government that was pioneered in England through the development of the powers of the English Parliament, even though the government of England, after 1668, was and remains a constitutional monarchy. In a sense, a parliamentary government is a government of parliamentary supremacy. It not only fuses the two branches, executive and legislative, it also puts the legislative over the executive in terms of power, since it is parliament that chooses the chief executive officer or prime minister. Not only that. Parliament also becomes the seat of both the executive and legislative branches.

The "presidential" form of government is termed so because of the presence of a president as the chief executive officer. Originally invented by the Founding Fathers, this form of government completely distinguished itself from that of England, which by then already did have a nascent parliamentary from of government. Thus one could literally say a presidential form of government is one with a president in the executive position, and a parliamentary is one with a prime minister in the executive position. Today, this can only be considered a "rule of thumb" that needs to be applied with caution, and needs to be elaborated on. Presidents are found in all three forms of government under discussion—presidential, parliamentary, and hybrid—but in each they have different functions and powers, from purely ceremonial to actual and formal. Thus, what originally was a good point of distinction, today is only a first step of comparison.

Just as the discussion of the territorial divisions in democracies points to the fact that these divisions have something to do with divisions of power within democracies, so also with the different forms of government, parliamentary and presidential. One way of looking at these different forms of government is to look at them as different degrees of concentration of power. Let us look at them the same way do we with territorial divisions, starting from the voters and their delegation of power through elections.

From the point of view of voters, a parliamentary form of government looks like this: voters elect their representatives to the legislature (parliament), and then have no more role to play in the selection of those individuals who will occupy the executive branch. Instead, parliament will turn around and select from among its elected representatives one who will serve as the chief executive officer or prime minister. When we say "parliament will turn around and select," we mean of course the chamber with the most power (in the case of bicameral parliaments). (For a discussion of bicameralism, see Chapter 7.) This chamber is usually called the lower house of parliament but, in fact, it holds the most power. The selection of the prime minister, again, is not made at random but, rather, the leader of the party or parties with the majority of the seats in that chamber tends to become prime minister. The decision is made by majority vote, and since the leader of the majority party has the majority of the votes, that person becomes prime minister. Once chosen prime minister that person continues to remain *in* parliament and votes *with* parliament. Being that he or she is also the leader of the majority in parliament *and* now also the chief executive officer, this person's wish becomes law almost automatically. A prime minister has formidable powers in comparison to a president, and a parliamentary form of government is one with a tremendous concentration of power in the hands of the executive. Now let us contrast this form of government with the presidential one.

Again, from the point of view of the voters, a presidential form of government looks like this: voters elect their representatives to their legislature but they also, and separately, elect their representative to the executive branch. This elected chief executive is called a president, and his powers are wholly independent of those of the legislature. The legislature, in turn, is wholly disconnected from the executive and has no say over who occupies that position. Being that they are both separated in this way, and both endowed with independent mandates for government, they both can speak for the people, but in order to do the business of government, they must cooperate. Typically, in presidential governments, the legislature and the president are constitutionally bound to act together in order to be able to legislate. A parliamentary system, of course, does not need such an extra provision as the legislature and the executive already function as one inside the parliament.

In terms of concentration of power, the presidential form of government is much weaker (i.e., less concentrated) than the parliamentary one, and this is by design. Founders of presidential forms of government distrust concentrations of power and want the people to have as many checks and balances on power as possible. (For a discussion of separation of powers and checks and balances see Chapter 7) If parliamentary systems are distinguished by *concentration* of power, presidential ones are distinguished by *fragmentation* of power. Prime examples of parliamentary and presidential forms of governments respectively are the government of England and that of the United States. They each invented their respective form of government. Technically speaking, however, the purest form of parliamentary government in Western Europe is not England but Germany, since England (or the United Kingdom, to be precise) is a constitutional monarchy that functions like a parliamentary system only with a hereditary monarch as head of state rather than an elected president as head of state and an elected prime minister as head of government.

Having mentioned the concepts of head of state and head of government respectively, it is well to briefly remark on these two concepts in the context of presidential and parliamentary government as well.

Parliamentary government can be distinguished from presidential government by focusing on the roles the executive must play or, to put it differently, the functions it must carry out. Typically, executives must carry out both the function of head of state and head of government. The head of state function is a ceremonial one, but being ceremonial it is no less important. In fact, ceremony and symbolism are essential to government, and we know this to be true when we observe the effect breaches of ceremony and protocol have on the body politic. I am particularly thinking of the moral failure of leaders when they are in office and the effects such failures have on the wellbeing of the entire nation even though moral uprightness is not a stated requirement for office in any democracy. The function of head of government, on the other hand, is the formal function of all executives, mandated by the constitutions of their respective countries and necessary for the day-to-day function of government.

Parliamentary and presidential governments can be distinguished on the notions of head of state and head of government. In parliamentary governments the position of head of state and that of head of government is held by two different persons whose job titles are "president" and "prime minister," respectively. As was already mentioned, prime ministers are usually elected indirectly in parliament. Presidents of parliamentary systems are also usually indirectly elected through the upper chambers of parliaments (if there are two chambers), but this need not be the case in all parliamentary systems and presidents can be elected directly by the people.

Presidential government, on the other hand, combines the functions of head of state and head of government in one and the same person. That person is elected by the people (either directly or via some version of an electoral college as in the United States), and his or her job title is "president." Presidential systems do not have a position of prime minister in their government structure, as this would be a redundant position given that the president already is head of government. The position of vice-president in a presidential system is not the equivalent of a prime minister's position. The vice-president is a "president-in-waiting," for lack of a better term, and until the vice-presidency of Dick Cheney under the George W. Bush presidency in the United States, the office was not much to write home about. With Dick Cheney, some say, the office has become almost equal in power to that of the president, but it is unlikely that the importance the office of the vice-president will continue beyond the present occupant, as American tradition requires it to be unobtrusive and unimportant.

Here we also see the obvious similarities between constitutional monarchies and parliamentary governments in that they are similar in all respects except that in constitutional monarchies the head of state is always an hereditary monarch and not an elected president.

Hybrid forms of government are combinations and permutations of presidential and parliamentary government specifically geared to the needs of that particular country. They exist because of historical developments that have led up to the current arrangement and are never found in the exact same combination in different countries. Examples of current hybrid forms are the government of France, that of Russia, and that of the nascent government of Iraq under American tutelage. Further technicalities aside, hybrids can be explained with the help of the notions of head of state and head of government mentioned earlier. Whereas parliamentary governments separate the functions of head of state and head of government and presidential ones unite them in the person of a president, hybrids give presidents both head of state and head of government functions (usually dealing with foreign policy and military matters as well as ceremonial matters) and assign prime ministers the function of head of government while denying them ceremonial tasks and making the position itself subject to presidential appointment with parliamentary approval. Under normal circumstances, therefore, prime ministers are chief bureaucrats only in hybrid systems, whereas presidents perform the tasks of "high politics."

CHAPTER 5

Territorial Divisions in Democracies

When speaking of democratic political systems, one needs to not only focus on their forms of government (republic, presidential, parliamentary, etc.) but also keep in mind the manner in which these political systems govern their territories. It is one thing for a system to be organized along this or that line, its representatives being elected this way or that way, and the relationship between its legislature and the executive being structured one way or the other. It is quite a different thing how that system, the center, interacts with the rest of the territory of the country, the periphery, of which it is the center, politically speaking. These differences in territorial divisions make, really, for different kinds of political systems, because a territorial division is also, in a way, a division of power, and how power is divided in a country ultimately makes a difference in the kind of political system the country has.

In democracies, territory can be governed in one of three ways: in unitary, confederate or federal fashion. Nondemocratic systems divide power—and thus govern their territory—only in one way, in unitary fashion, by definition. What is the difference between these three territorial divisions and what is the rationale behind them? Some territorial divisions are better suited to some countries than other types of territorial divisions. The reason may have to do with history or size or diversity or homogeneity or a combination of some or all of these factors.

Unitary territorial divisions are best suited to countries that are not too large, not too diverse in populations and regions and cultures, and have had a history of government from the center to which the people are accustomed. Confederate territorial divisions are typically transitional territorial divisions or arrangements of convenience of a temporary but not long-term kind. They are particularly suitable for areas where previously independent entities seek to come together as a unified entity, or where stronger arrangements are not politically feasible at that time. Existing and historical examples of confederations all show the limitations of this territorial organization. Yet, the rationale for their existence will translate into more such confederations forming on the world scene whenever groups of formerly independent or newly independent countries or regions will seek to come together. Federation, on the other hand, is the best solution for large-scale entities that have diverse regions or cultures that need to be given some form of autonomy and political recognition but who also do not want to deteriorate into the centrifugal vortex that confederations represent. Typically, federations have formed as a result of the collapse of the confederate experiment (the United States) or the collapse of the former unitary experiment (Germany and Russia today).

From the point of view of concentration of power, the unitary territorial division is the most concentrated at the center, the confederate one is the least concentrated at the center and thus most concentrated at the periphery, and the federal territorial division is a compromise between the two, with a slight advantage to the center in order to keep it from collapsing into, or reverting back to a confederation. The centrifugal force is still strong, and some might say by design, in a federation.

What do the three territorial divisions look like from the point of view of the voters? (We choose this vantage point because in democracies the voters are the beginning of the democratic process and the sovereign source of power.) In a unitary system, voters elect their representatives at the center (for the legislature and the executive), then they have no more role to play (i.e., they have no further role in deciding who governs in their name at the periphery). The governors of the periphery are chosen or selected by the representatives at the center, and those governors answer to the elected representatives at the center and carry out their will at the periphery.

In a confederation, the above order is reversed. The people elect their representatives at the periphery and then have no further role to play in the selection of those who will govern or, rather, manage the center. The latter are selected by the representatives at the periphery and answer to them.

In a federal system, voters elect *both* their representatives at the center and at the periphery. Then both these arenas work together as equals in administering the affairs of the country. To resolve possible disputes that might arise, however, a federal system does give the center slightly more power than the periphery but only in cases where a question relating to the country as a whole might be at stake. This is the spirit of the phrase of the second paragraph of Article VI of the U.S. Constitution known as the "supremacy clause." All federal systems include such a "clause" somewhere in their constitutions. Without such a clause, two possible scenarios might prevail: one, disputes could not be resolved thus leading to stalemate; two, the system would revert to confederation due to the pressure from the constituent units, the states.

Next we need to shift gears to a different discussion, away from a typology of governments to a discussion of the underlying principles of the U.S. Constitution. To complete this discussion, however, it is well to also look at the three additional seminal documents that have helped shape today's political system in the United States.

Part II: Process

CHAPTER 6

Documents of Democracy

The American political experience, like all other political experiences, is not *sui generis*. It has antecedents in both Europe and North America, and one way to trace the genesis of the American experiment is to look at the documents that inform that experience.

Although they had left for reasons of religious intolerance at home, by 1620, when the Pilgrims landed near Plymouth, the British people had been beneficiaries of almost four centuries of political developments, giving them gradually greater and greater rights. This slow process of devolution of power to the people had started with the signing of the Magna Carta (the Great Charter) by King John in 1215, and continued beyond the arrival of the early settlers in America to the Glorious Revolution of 1688 and the English Bill of Rights of 1689, consolidating once and for all a monarchy limited by a parliament and a people endowed with guarantees against abuse.

What in American textbooks is referred to as the British legal tradition starts with the rights granted in the Great Charter by King John. Though originally applicable only to nobles (the English barons), of course, the right of "trial by a jury of peers" and the principle of *habeas corpus* granted in the Magna Carta have become bedrock principles manifest in the U.S. Constitution in Article I, section 9, and the Fourth and Eighth amendments of the U.S. Bill of Rights. Furthermore, the practice of British judges "riding the circuit" to dispense justice, based on the principle of *habeas corpus* and the prohibition in the Magna Carta that officials of the crown may not try individuals for crimes, also gives rise in name and form to many judicial practices in the United States, such as the existence of the Circuit Courts of Appeal that are the intermediary tier of twelve courts on the federal side are to which cases can be appealed before being appealed one last time to the U.S. Supreme Court itself.

Habeas corpus is a medieval Latin phrase literally meaning "you have the body," issued as a command to the jailor by a judge. It is in reference to the power of judges to ask the jailor to bring a prisoner before them and to ask why the prisoner was held in the first place. The principle also implied that if the judge could not be satisfied that the prisoner was held for sound juridical reasons, the prisoner would have to be freed. *Habeas corpus* was issued as a writ and is known as the "Great Writ" in legal tradition, and is referred to as "the writ of *habeas corpus*" in Article I, section 9 of the U.S. Constitution. Though mentioned in the body of the U.S. Constitution, *habeas corpus* is not an absolute right. The British and U.S. legal traditions acknowledge that the writ of *habeas corpus* can be suspended in times of "rebellion or invasion" when the public safety may require it, but this suspension, scholars argue, would be the prerogative of the legislative branch and not that of the executive. In support of this interpretation, the supreme covet in *Hamdi v. Rumsfeld* (USSC, 03-6696, June 2004) held that U.S. citizens could not be denied *habeas corpus*. The current case of *Boumediene v. Bush* (USSC, 06-1195, June 2008) decided that *habeas corpus* applied to foreign detainees as well, and though the Military Commissions Act of 2006 had given the president the power to detain and forcefully interrogate persons termed "enemy combatants," the U.S. Supreme Court in *Hamdan v. Rumsfeld* (USSC, 05-184, June 2006) still tied the hands of the president by declaring military commissions unconstitutional.

The Declaration of Independence (see Appendix B) is the first great American statement of principles that informs the American political experience. Issued in the context of the struggle of the colonists and the oppression and tyranny of England, the Declaration spells out key principles of American politics. In essence, it is closer to the Magna Carta than the Articles of Confederation or the Constitution, as it is in fact not a constitution but a statement of principles and a repository of the rights of peoples.

The first two paragraphs of the Declaration assert the right to revolution against unjust government, the "self-evidence" of the equality of all men, the existence of "certain unalienable rights" such as the right to "life, liberty, and the pursuit of Happiness," and the legitimacy of government based on the notion of "consent of the governed" rather than that of divine right which was the basis of the claim of legitimacy of kings. Since the Declaration is not a constitution but rather a statement of principles, its principles are found reflected in the Constitution of the United States.

The principle of the legitimacy of government by consent of the governed makes possible both the political systems under the Articles of Confederation and under the U.S. Constitution. The notion of equality is reflected both in the principle of political equality ("one person, one vote"), but also specifically in the great phrase of the Fourteenth Amendment that no state shall deny any person "the equal protection of the laws" (Amend. XIV, section 1). Finally, though not repeated with the same flourish as Jefferson's formulation of it, John Locke's phrase "life, liberty, and property" from his Second Treatise of Government (1690) made its way into the U.S. Constitution in the Fifth and Fourteenth amendments.

The Articles of Confederation (1777/1781) were the first constitution of the United States. Though they did not specifically refer to any of the principles spoken of earlier, they embodied of course the notion of government by consent of the government, since they established a representative democracy. They also, for the first time, addressed the question of territorial organization of the United States.

As was mentioned above, the Magna Carta and the Declaration of Independence were repositories of rights and not constitutions. They thus fulfilled part of what constitutions are intended to do as limits on the power of government, but it was not within their scope to do more. Constitutions must, in addition to limiting power, be blueprints for governance. It is for this reason that they outline the powers and shapes of the branches of government and the manner in which the territory over which the government is established is to be governed. The Articles of Confederation adopted by the Second Continental Congress in 1777 and finally ratified in 1781, fulfilled for the United States this second aspect of constitutions, that of being their first blueprint of government.

In declaring themselves independent of England the colonialists had to also create a new political system to govern them, thus they transitioned from autocratic rule to democratic rule as Jefferson makes clear in the Declaration of Independence, but they chose one specific form of democratic government over the other available alternatives, confederation. There is a great deal of speculation as to why confederation was chosen over the available alternatives, but the choice of the founders becomes clearer if one recalls for a moment what the alternatives were in 1776.

From our vantage point today a great variety of forms of government (i.e., political systems) are available to choose from, but we need to think back to the time before the American Revolution to see that the choice for the Founders was limited only to either absolute monarchy or constitutional monarchy if the Founders were to consider only contemporary types of rule. If they were to look back to history, they would find republics, more or less on the Roman model, and democracies more or less on the Athenian model also as guides. Here then was the dilemma as they saw it: They wished for popular government (i.e., government by popular sovereignty) but they did not wish to duplicate it along Athenian lines. For better or worse they were the equivalent of landed aristocracy (minus the hereditary implication that the term carried with it in Europe) and for better or worse also, they trusted the impulses that came with this tie to the land more than any other impulses that might arise in popular government. A republican form of government (i.e., government through elected representatives) was therefore the only acceptable alternative, but that was only half the answer they were seeking. The other half was how to govern as diverse a group as the thirteen newly minted independent states as one rather than thirteen different countries. For so complicated an arrangement there was no obvious model to follow.

Only two relevant precedents existed from which the Founders could possibly choose. One was the precedent of the Old Swiss Confederacy dating back to the high Middle Ages. It would stand to reason that the Founders would have been familiar with this experiment since they were steeped in European history and familiar with the works of Europe's most famous "Swiss" thinkers, John Calvin and Jean-Jacques Rousseau. Yet, there is no evidence that the Swiss Confederation was considered at all by the Founders. What was considered was closer to home and the evidence for it is now fairly uncontested, namely, the confederation of the

Iroquois nations, which Benjamin Franklin had studied for years and was avidly recommending as a model to follow for the soon to be ex-colonies of England.

The appeal of a confederation was perfect in that it embraced independence while adding union, a felicitous marriage of convenience serving both the purpose of unity against a potential new adversary, England, and individuality for all the newly independent entities (the states) who would be guarding that newfound freedom jealously. Indeed, that was exactly the option chosen as confederation provided the additional benefit of complementing well the notion of democracy in contradistinction to the hated colonial overlordship that the Founders were trying to move away from. Looking at it from this perspective two aims were achieved with the combination of confederation and representative democracy: both are polar opposites of the power concentration absolute monarchy represents and thus made perfect sense in view of what it was the Founders intended to achieve, namely anything but duplicating England!

Despite satisfying the immediate needs of the states after their declaration of independence from England, the Articles quickly proved inadequate in addressing the complexities of governance that came with this new form of government. Two main shortcomings became evident immediately: the new government had no power of taxation and the new government was paralyzed by the requirement of unanimous consent in Article XIII. These inadequacies combined with the perpetual threat of military defeat to England created a sufficient sense of urgency to seek to remedy the shortcomings of the Articles. The resulting efforts would culminate in the Constitutional Convention of Philadelphia in the summer of 1787 and the creation of a completely new document and political system, a new federal republic with the U.S. Constitution as its foundation.

CHAPTER 7

Principles of the U.S. Constitution

There are several core principles embodied in every constitution that form the basis or foundation upon which that constitution is built. In the American context, these core principles are republicanism, bicameralism, federalism, separation of powers, checks and balances, and constitutionalism itself. Of these, the core principles are the ones discussed below:

BICAMERALISM

Bicameralism is a term that has reference only in the context of legislative chambers. Literally, the term "bicameral" refers to the existence of two chambers in a legislature as opposed to only one chamber, in which case the legislature would be referred to as "unicameral." Bicameral legislatures are more common than unicameral ones, but frequency is not an indication of superiority, necessarily, but rather of political exigency and need. There is also, of course, the question of history, and the fact that many subsequently established legislatures took as the model to emulate either the British or the French or the American legislatures, all of which are bicameral. There are some notable exceptions though, such as the legislature of Israel, the Knesset, which, though based on the British model of government, is a unicameral legislature, or that of the emerging European Union, whose parliament is unicameral also.

Bicameralism is not the same as bicameral. It is more than that. While bicameral refers to a geographical or architectural arrangement, bicameralism refers to a legislative practice, a way of legislating that involves both legislative chambers with some form of distribution of power among them. Often this distribution of power between the legislative chambers is not equal. To distinguish between equally distributed powers in both chambers and unequal distribution, the qualifiers "symmetrical" and "asymmetrical" are added for the purpose of clarification and precision. Very few legislatures in the world have perfectly symmetrical bicameral legislatures. The norm is asymmetry in varying degrees, from slight asymmetries like those of the legislature of France or Italy, to more severe ones like that of England, where, for all practical purposes, one is approaching a unicameral situation with a historical relic remaining as a reminder of a former political arrangement, the House of Lords.

The world's first and still *only* perfectly symmetrical bicameral legislature is that of the United States. As with the presidential form of government and the federal territorial division, a perfectly symmetrical bicameral legislature is a genuine American invention and contribution to the world of politics.

Bicameralism is reflected in the U.S. Constitution in several places, both in terms of its literal meaning of two chambers in the legislature, as well as in terms of the idea of equal distribution of power between the two chambers. As to the mention of two chambers, Article I, section 1, of the U.S. Constitution states that the legislative power shall be vested in a Congress composed of the House of Representatives and the Senate, thus giving us the legal basis for a two-chambered legislature. Article I, section 7, however, lays the groundwork for the equal distribution of power between the two chambers when it states that "every bill, which shall have passed the House of Representatives and the Senate, shall, before it become a law, be presented to the President of the United States." This injunction makes clear that no bill can become law unless *both* the House and the Senate have passed it, and thus indicates the perfect power symmetry of both chambers.

The origin of this symmetry in the U.S. legislature goes back to the Connecticut or Great Compromise of 1787. The exigency of having to accommodate different sized states with different needs, led to a two-chambered legislature, with each chamber serving the needs of one set of states, but with neither chamber having more power than the other. Thus was born symmetrical bicameralism in America.

SEPARATION OF POWERS AND CHECKS AND BALANCES

Separation of powers and checks and balances are the two principles that are most essential to the functioning of the American government. The following points will make clear the importance and place of these principles in the U.S. Constitution and in the day-to-day governance of the United States.

Separation of powers and checks and balances are called the "twin principles" of the Constitution. The reason is that you cannot have one without the other. (This will become clear from the points below.) The term "separation of powers" is a specific term in political science. It refers *only* to the act of separating the powers of government. It does not refer to things like the division of power between the states and the national government under a federal arrangement.

Government is a complex entity made up of three branches or powers, each performing different functions. Together these three branches enable government to perform its function of policy making. All governments, democratic and nondemocratic alike, have these three branches and the three branches perform their respective functions of legislation, execution, and adjudication. However, only democratic government has its three branches operating independently from each other, and thus only democratic government is the kind of government in which people feel free from possible governmental abuse of power.

The notion of the powers of government and their proper relationship to each other comes to us from the political and philosophical debate of seventeenth- and eighteenth-century Europe. Europe was governed by absolute monarchies during that period. Absolute monarchy is a system of governance that concentrates the three powers of government in the hand of the monarch *and* in which there is no appeal to the will or edict of that monarch. As if this was not already strong enough, absolute monarchy also supported itself and its right to govern with a further theory called "divine right," which stated that the monarch has the right to rule the way he does because that is the will of God.

Philosophers in the seventeenth and eighteenth century argued against this principle of absolute monarchy and against the theory of legitimacy that sustained it, divine right. These philosophers came to be known as the social contract theorists. They were Thomas Hobbes, John Locke, and Jean-Jacques Rousseau. John Locke's ideas are the most relevant here. The American Founding Fathers followed him not the other two.

John Locke argued that monarchical government cannot justify itself on the notion of divine right because absolute monarchies are patently unjust and unfair. Unless we hold that God decrees injustice, the argument for divine right of absolute monarchs becomes weak. He further argued that what was wrong with absolute monarchy was the concentration of the three powers of government in the hands of one person to whose will there was no appeal. Thus he suggested that 1) the powers of government be split up (separation of powers); 2) that the legislative power be placed in the hands of the people through their representatives (elected parliament); and 3) that the executive power/branch be made subject to the laws made by the legislative, on the principle that "no one is above the law." This, he argued, would enable one to achieve fair government with regard to the people. John Locke also added that the theory that should sustain this new form of government (which we today call representative democracy) should be "consent of the governed" instead of "divine right." Consent of the governed means that government is only legitimate if the people agree to being governed by it.

Thus, we have the following four alternative forms of government, from the kind of government in which people have the least say to the kind where they have the most say:

1) absolute monarchy

2) constitutional or limited monarchy

3) representative democracy or "republic"

4) direct democracy

The American Founding Fathers chose "representative democracy" as their preferred form of government. They did not want monarchy at all, even in its limited fashion, nor did they want too much democracy in the form of direct democracy. Thus the notion of separation of powers, which leads to the philosophical and political debate listed above, lead them to adopt a middle position between too little power to the people and too much.

If one were to separate the three powers of government without building in "links" between them after separating them, one would get three independent branches with no means of governing (they would cancel each other out). Thus after separating them to safeguard the people from harm, one needs to build in "oversight" by one branch over the other in order to get even fairer government. Not only does separation of powers give us protection from a potentially abusive executive branch, checks and balances gives us also a further way by which the legislative can "check" the power of the executive, and also for the democratically elected executive to now check a too eager legislative, and so forth.

In the American context this equilibrium resulting from the application of the principles of separation of power and checks and balances is called the "Madisonian system," after James Madison, the founding father who is most associated with it. He reasoned that the quest for self-interest of each branch, counterbalanced by that of the other branches, results in the kind of government where the people are safe from abuse of power. (See Federalist No. 51, Appendix D). In the U.S. Constitution, the powers of Congress to check the executive are listed in Article II, section 2. The power of the executive to check the legislature is listed in Article I, section 7. The power of the Court to check both is not found in the constitution but was argued by Chief Justice John Marshall to derive from the mandate of the court in the case *Marbury v. Madison* (1803). (See Appendix E). Both Congress and the executive have expanded their powers to check the other branches by arguing for "implied powers" in the constitution. Thus the president has claimed for himself the power to issue executive orders and agreements; Congress at one point claimed the privilege of the "legislative veto" and, of course, the Court has claimed the power of "judicial review."

FEDERALISM

The term "federalism" should not be confused with the term "federal" (i.e., territorial division). The two are of course related terms, but "federalism" implies ways in which the federal structure is applied, whereas "federal" simply describes the structure itself. Let us clarify that point a little more.

The implication in the federal territorial division is that there are different levels of government, the national or federal, the state, and the local levels. This notion of levels of government is given in each of the territorial divisions. What distinguishes the federal one from the others is the fact that in the federal territorial division there is one more level or layer of government than in any of the other ones. This notion of "levels of government" is crucial to the term federalism. Federalism primarily implies a *relationship* between the different levels of government that is directed not only from the center, but also from the periphery or the states and local governments. It is a mutual relationship between these levels of government. The textbook definition of federalism is "the exercise of power by two or more governments over the same people or territory." The relationship between these levels of government is best described in what are termed "phases of federalism."

The first phase of this relationship can be described as one of "live and let live." It is known as dual federalism and lasted from the founding of the republic to about 1930. From 1930 onward, the new phase is called "cooperative federalism," and characterized by national government involvement in solving the nation's problems and its attempt to set national standards and ensure uniform application of benefits. This trend, starting in the New Deal era, continues through President Lyndon Johnson's Great Society era of the mid-1960s. It is characterized by the availability of money at the federal level and a willingness to spend the money on large government programs such as the War on Poverty. With the advent of the Nixon presidency and the last years of the Vietnam War, the mood of the nation changes, though at first, monies are still plentifully available. President Nixon ushers in the new phase of federalism termed "new federalism." This new federalism is distinguished from the old by the introduction of revenue sharing and by the use of more and more block grants to give states more independence from Washington. President Nixon's new federalism is continued by President Reagan's new federalism in the1980s. Some termed this phase "new new federalism." The difference between President Reagan's new federalism and that of President Nixon had to do with the willingness of Washington to spend money and the availability of it. President Reagan's new federalism also used block grants, but there was less money available, leaving the states to fend for themselves when it came to demands from the people for services and programs they felt they were entitled to. The next phase of federalism was that of the republican ascendancy under President Clinton's presidency, the era of Representative Newt Gingrich, who later became the powerful Speaker of the House of Representatives with the Republican majority he had engineered. Some have referred to this period as "Newt federalism." This period of federalism distinguished itself by more cutbacks in programs from the national level and a greater willingness still to use block grants to enable the states to use them for their own purposes. This willingness to rely on states went hand in hand with a distrust of "Washington," an odd sentiment coming from the very people who occupied the seats of power in it!

With the advent of September 11, 2001, we entered into a new phase of federalism distinguished by a marked increase in national government power and a centralization of that power with the central government at the expense of the states due to security imperatives. This new phase was ushered in with the passage of the USA Patriot Act in October 2001 and of the Homeland Security Act in November 2002 and with the creation of the largest federal bureaucracy to date, the Department of Homeland Security.

In 2008 we are still in this phase of federalism. One thing that this development shows us is that federalism in America has swung back and forth like a pendulum.

Now that the pendulum has swung so strongly to the side of national government power, it stands to reason that the next type of federalism will be a more gradual approach back to the states.

There is another way of looking at the relationship between the national level of government and that of the states and localities, and that has to do with the kind of relationship it is. It is in the nature of every central or national government to try to assert its superiority and sovereignty. One sign of the superiority or sovereignty of the national government over the states and localities is the power of the national government to tax. The flow of money from the state and localities to the national government and back again to them based on the national government's priorities is called "fiscal federalism" in the literature. Fiscal federalism describes a relationship of power between the states and the national government, in which the national government has the upper hand, as the states do not get to tax the national government, but the national government gets to tax the residents of the states. The U.S. Supreme Court case that settled this issue of who gets to tax whom is the famous case of *McCulloch v. Maryland* (1819). (See Appendix F for text of *McCulloch v. Maryland*.)

Fiscal federalism describes the nature of the tax relationship between the federal government and the states, and shows how the national government over time has interpreted its role in this relationship. While the power to collect income tax exists in reality only since 1913 with the adoption of the Sixteenth Amendment, the relationship has changed over time. During the height of the New Deal legislation in the 1930s and early 1940s, the fiscal relationship between the federal government and the states and localities was one in which the federal government mandated exactly how "federal" dollars were to be spent that were sent back to the states. In the 1970s, 1980s, and 1990s, that relationship changed more and more to letting the states decide how those dollars were spent, even to the extreme of barring the national government from mandating expenses for the states unless it gave them the money to do so. This was the provision of the "unfunded mandates" of the Contract with America of 1994.

This fiscal relationship has been described with various names given to the monies that flow from Washington to the states and describing the presence or absence of strings attached thereto. The general term describing this relationship is "revenue sharing," though there is a specific meaning to the term that has to do with its application to the states under the presidency of Richard Nixon in the early 1970s. Revenue sharing manifested itself as either "general revenue sharing," which meant money provided to the states to be used with very few "strings attached" or restrictions, and "special revenue sharing," which meant that monies would be given to the states in the form of grants. There are two forms of grants through which monies are given to the states: categorical or formula grants, which state specifically how and where the money is to be spent, and block grants, which have no strings attached and leave the states and localities free to spend the money where they see fit and need it most. States prefer block grants obviously because of the leeway it gives them on how to spend the money. The national government often prefers the categorical grants because it gives it an opportunity to shape the nation in a certain direction. This debate has a very contemporary component to it when it comes to funds for education, for instance under the policy of "No child left Behind." (No child left Behind Act of 2001). Generally speaking, conservatives like block grants because of their philosophy that the states should have maximum say in their own sphere of influence (a position called "states rights"). Liberals, on the other hand, prefer categorical grants, as it gives them an opportunity to steer things from the center and assures them of the fact that there is a uniform application of benefits nation-wide. These two views on these matters make for the debate on federalism, and as every student of politics knows, now the conservative view has the upper hand and the conservative view has moved away from states rights in all matters to using the national government power to influence issues along ideological lines. This goes to show that the positions of the left and the right are not rigidly in favor of one or the other application of national government power.

Federalism can also be explained through the use of models and over time three models describing the relationship between the center and the periphery in a federal structure have emerged. These models are called layer-cake, marble-cake, and picket-fence. (The use of kitchen recipe terms is incidental here, but somehow preferred by the authors of these models. There have also been other terms bandied about that further reflect the culinary arts such as "tossed-salad federalism" and the one that takes the cake—no pun intended!—"fruitcake federalism." We will get back to the possible meanings of these terms below.) Layer-cake, marble-cake and picket-fence, all describe relationships between the national and state and local levels that are termed, respectively, dual federalism and cooperative federalism. Let us turn to each of these models and the relationships they describe.

The layer-cake model is a description of the type of federalism called dual federalism. Dual federalism holds that the national and state levels of government operate strictly side by side with minimal, if any, interference and overlap. It further holds that each level of government is sovereign in its sphere and that the two "layers" are distinct and separate as are those of the cake by that same name. The idea that is being conveyed here is that of a territory run along two parallel lines with little interference from one sphere into the affairs of the other. How accurate a description of the actuality of things is this model? Political scientists feel that this model describes some of the reality of the relationship between the national government and the states; they also feel that the U.S. Constitution bears out some of this interpretation in passages such as the Tenth Amendment to the Constitution, or in the language of Article IV of the Constitution, but that overall, this is too exaggerated a description and not reflective of the dynamic interrelationship between the national government and the states and localities.

There is one period in the history of the United States, however, that does correspond to the way this model views the relationship between the national government and the states and localities, and that period is the period of the founding of this nation to perhaps the beginning of the twentieth century. There is a very good reason why the relationship between the national government and the states was like this during that period. It had to do with distance and with technology. During the early days of the republic and the period of westward expansion, from the Louisiana Purchase onward, the federal government was in no position to "micromanage" the development of the nation. The nation was too vast, and Washington, D.C., too remote. The idea of "live and let live" was a practical and pragmatic response to the exigencies of the day. The federal government would only intervene in the most egregious cases and only when it felt that the interests of the nation as a whole would otherwise be threatened. This type of relationship even continued after the defeat of the southern states in the Civil War and the period of reconstruction that followed, as evidenced by the U.S. Supreme Court's decision in *Plessy v. Ferguson* (1896), the essence of which was to leave the states free to interpret the constitution differently than the national government. (See Appendix I for text of *Plessy v. Ferguson*.)

There is general agreement that the period of dual federalism ended with the Great Depression (1930) and the involvement of the government in national affairs with the beginning of the New Deal. The federalism model that best describes the period that begins in the 1930s and continues on to the 1970s is called marble cake. The name for that period is cooperative federalism, but the term has much wider application than just a description for that period in American history.

Unlike layer-cake, marble-cake federalism holds that the two levels of national and state and locality are intricately intertwined and that it is difficult to say where the national government ends and where the states begin. Marble-cake federalism derives its name from the cake in which the vanilla and chocolate parts are so mixed up that separating them is a truly impossible task. Marble-cake federalism does not deny that the different levels of government are each sovereign in their own spheres, it just holds that the spheres are not as rigidly separate as the other model holds, and that there are substantial overlaps between the two. In that, this model of federalism is a much more accurate description of the reality of federalism than the previous one, for in truth, it is very difficult to tell in every day life, where the national government ends and where the state and local governments begin. The simple example of the overlapping jurisdictions of law enforcement on the national highways (freeways) is a very good reminder of that fact. If one exceeds the speed limit on a national highway while driving through a city, national, state, county, or city law enforcement officers could stop one and co-operate in stopping one if need be. City police and county sheriffs could also pursue a suspect beyond their respective government limits on the freeway if need be, and would be well within their rights to stop a suspect beyond their respective municipal and county boundaries.

Cooperative federalism also derives its legitimacy from the U.S. Constitution and an interpretation of the various clauses of the Constitution that give the national government the right to intervene in the affairs of the states such as the powers granted to the national government (Congress in this case) in Article I, section 8.

From the mid-1970s onward the relationship between the national government and the states and localities changes once more, not perhaps in kind so much as in quality. While cooperative federalism remains the more descriptive model of the two, a more dynamic model called "picket-fence federalism" better describes the actuality of the relationships between the three levels of government involved.

Picket-fence federalism holds that the relationship between the three levels of government must be seen in terms of the issues and policies that bind them together. While the three levels of government form the horizontal slats of the fence, the vertical posts and planks are the issues and policies that link the three levels together, in that they affect individuals and decision-makers residing at all three levels. Take for instance, education, as one of these planks. The issue of education is both a national, a state and a local one, and all three levels of government as well as the individuals dealing with this issue at al three levels are involved in the decision-making process. Picket-fence federalism holds that the three levels of government work together in this dynamic fashion to address the problems the nation faces and it points to the fact that there is a continuous flow of influence from the local level to the state and to the national level and vice-versa. The interesting aspect of this model is also that it points to the element in the political system that furthers this flow of influence from the national level to the state and local and back up again, and that element, in this political system of ours is the interest groups. (More on that in the lectures on interest groups and the political system).

One last word about kitchen recipes. What was the meaning of those terms we used earlier, "tossed-salad federalism" and "fruitcake federalism"? Tossed salad federalism meant to extend the metaphor of marble cake federalism one step further by pointing to the wild mix of the different levels and perhaps to the fact that there is no pattern as to which level of government would prevail where. Fruitcake federalism has been described by Kenneth Janda et al., as "a federalism that is formless and indestructible, and offers lots of plums for everyone." Oh well, so much for political scientists and kitchen recipes!

CHAPTER 8

Socialization, Political Opinion and Participation

This segment deals with the link between the notions of socialization, political opinion, and participation. It attempts to show that there is a connection among socialization, political opinion building, and levels and kinds of participation. We have already encountered the notion of socialization as part of our discussion of the political system, now let us look at it in terms of its relation to the other two terms of political opinion and political participation.

Generally speaking, socialization is a societal phenomenon. It is a process by which the members of a society inculcate their values in the next generation in order to ensure the survival of that society. As such, this process is automatic. It is also unconscious, in the sense that there is no organized and concerted effort called "socialization" other than in the textbooks of social scientists, that society engages in at a certain given moment in time. Socialization is also ongoing. It is a constant process going on from generation to generation resulting in the continued success of that society in maintaining itself and its norms and values intact.

Society achieves the socialization of its members by a variety of means and through a variety of agencies or agents of socialization. These agents are the same for socialization as they are for the more specific process of political socialization, that is, society's way of turning its members into active and supportive *citizens*. Agents of socialization inculcate in the members of society the values and norms of that society. When they act as agents of political socialization, they inculcate in those that are affected by them the values of citizenship and participation.

The agents of socialization are first the family, then school, peers, the media, religious organizations, voluntary associations such as clubs and the like, one's job, and, finally, government and the other institutions of the political system itself. Each of these institutions or agents, in turn plays the double role of teaching the newer members of that society the dos and don'ts of that society, but also, somewhere along the line influence and teach adherence to the political system and the institution of government.

This process of political socialization starts early, in the home, where children hear from parents and other extended members of the family what the proper response to "the government" or "the president" or "the flag" or "the Constitution" or "the police" is. In school, teachers are mandated to teach children about "their country," "their flag," their presidents" etc. To a lesser degree at first, but then to a greater and greater degree, peers influence these attitudes further. All along, the media shape the images we associate with government and guide us in acquiring our first notions of what will ultimately become our political opinions. Later in life, our jobs and our peers at work play a crucial role in shaping and maintaining our beliefs in the political system and its institutions. Lastly, government itself, with its ubiquitous presence in the form of the president or Congress or, to a lesser degree, the Supreme Court, influences and guides us in our views, and inculcates in us a sense of patriotism, duty, belonging and loyalty.

As a result of this ongoing and complex process, political views are generated in us, which over time and with reinforcement from our own experience, become the political opinions we will hold later in life. When analyzing these opinions, political scientists categorize them along a spectrum of ideologies, which includes all the possible political points of view that are organized in coherent and all-encompassing form, called ideologies. These ideologies are said to span the spectrum from left to right, and include prominently in America the ideologies of liberalism and conservatism.

Today, both these ideologies can be called "centrist," meaning that they are both very close to the moderate center of the political spectrum, while still exhibiting marked differences in their core beliefs however. Generally, liberals tend to favor government intervention in the economy to help those that are on the lower end of the economic ladder. This they want to achieve through progressive taxation and government programs designed to help the middle class and the poor. Their constituency is typically minorities (economic, gender, and racial), labor unions, a large portion of the retired population, and generally a large portion of the working and middle classes. But they do not exclusively speak for these populations. Liberals have expanded their appeal to upper middle class and business as well, even though with less success than the conservatives for whom these populations are the natural constituency, but again, not exclusively.

Today conservatives tend to divide into social, on the one hand, and economic conservatives on the other. Social conservatives tend to emphasize traditional values of family, God and country, but within this framework some of them tend to be more zealous for one or the cause such as opposition to abortion rights, or favoring prayer in school, or opposition to gay rights. Economic conservatives tend to favor as free an economy as possible. They embrace the notions of free trade and free markets, the most significant feature of which is the absence of government intervention in the activities of individuals and companies in the form of absence of regulation and taxation as much as possible.

Like conservatives, liberals also split into social and economic camps. While their economic and political views are outlined above as favoring government intervention to remedy economic imbalances, on the social front liberals tend to favor a "hands-off" approach. They feel government should stay out of the lives of people and not try to influence behavior through mandating prayer in schools and the like.

As we are exposed to these views through the agencies of socialization in our formative years, we inevitably tend to adopt one or the other position, and, over time, build a more or less coherent political opinion that could be characterized as either conservative or liberal in most instances. Few, however, are strictly in one camp or the other at all times, and most people will find that they are somewhere in between these two views depending on the issue at hand, or depending on where they are in their lives, careers, and years. Age and experience tend to change even the most dearly held beliefs at some point, but then again, not always.

The transition from political opinions to political participation is a natural one. Political opinions direct us toward involvement with the political system. We realize that to achieve our aims we need to and can let the system know what we feel. We also realize that we can get it to respond in support of our views if we are able to put our views in such a way that the system can hear us. Thus, participation occurs at a variety of levels and in a variety of forms, each in progressive degrees trying to achieve our aim of having our views put into practice by the political system in the form of policies we favor.

Political participation is the citizen's attempt to influence the outcome of the political process. Participation occurs in a variety of ways we call "kinds" of participation. Participation also occurs in different degrees. This is what is called "levels" of participation. Both levels and kinds of participation are determined by the level and kind of socialization we have undergone in our formative years and still undergo at present. Participation also, of course, is influenced by the political beliefs we hold, by our political opinions.

There are four kinds of political participation:

conventional/supportive

nonparticipation

unconventional/nonsupportive

violent opposition

Of these four, three are accommodated through democratic political systems. They are the essence of democracy. No political system, however, democratic or nondemocratic, will tolerate the fourth kind of participation, as it is meant to challenge the very existence of that system and all systems are inherently geared to see to their own survival. The difference between democratic and nondemocratic systems is still going to be in the limits they impose on themselves even while dealing with violent opposition. Democratic systems are bound by the limits of civilized behavior and must answer to laws that take into consideration the rights of people regardless of the circumstance in which they find themselves. Nondemocratic systems do not feel bound by these restraints, and thus deal with violent opposition without any internal restraint.

Except for the last category of participation, the other three are common in democratic systems. Conventional participation is the kind of participation that engages citizens in the most benign activities in support of the system. In America, that would mean voting, distributing voter registration pamphlets, registering voters, calling representatives, signing petitions, etc.

It may seem strange to list nonparticipation as a kind of participation but, as a matter of fact, nonparticipation is also a kind of participation, namely, the decision *not to participate*. There are a variety of reasons why people do not participate in the political process, dislike of the process, lack of information, feeling of helplessness, sheer laziness, unawareness that there is a process or that there is a need to participate in it, etc. Whatever the reason may be, the act of nonparticipation is a kind of participation, a decision that, except in the extreme case of unawareness of the entire process, is a conscious one of not participating instead of participating. For this reason, nonparticipation is considered a kind of participation. Fully 45–50 percent of Americans exercise that option during presidential elections, and 60 percent or more exercise that option every two years in midterm House and Senate elections.

Unconventional or nonconventional participation is the kind of participation some have called "civil disobedience." It entails demonstrating dissatisfaction with the political system by a variety of means that reach almost all the way up to violent opposition but do not cross that line. The distinction is clear in most cases. Political assassination, the use of firearms and explosives, kidnapping, hijacking, extortion, hostage-taking, these are clear acts of violence that no state needs to tolerate. However, democratic political systems must tolerate demonstrations, even when they turn a bit rough. They must tolerate rallies, marches, sit-ins, disruptions of one kind or another of this sort, let alone those that are expressly protected by the constitution, such as speeches that are antagonistic to the system, flag burnings, antiwar publications in journals and newspapers, and so on. Of course, it must tolerate and protect the rights of citizens to simply disagree, which is the mildest form of nonconventional participation.

Some political scientists have suggested that there is an order of preference indicated here in the four types of participation listed, and that modern democratic political systems tend to socialize people so that they would engage in conventional participation or alternately in nonparticipation. The reason for this is that both those types of participation help keep the system stable without any dramatic changes and ensure that the same people, more or less, remain in power. The high rate of reelection and the phenomenon of incumbency in the elected positions and the recurrence of the same names in the non-elective positions within the system seem to support that contention. However, this may just as much be by default as by design. There is universal agreement, however, that systems do not like opposition not even of the kind that we called nonconventional participation, and that they would rather avoid this altogether if they could. Democratic political systems, however, have no choice in the matter, and in a sense must even offer the option to their citizens by educating them about it.

Lastly, the notion of levels of participation. The more successfully socialized an individual is, and the more that socialization has encouraged conventional participation, the more likely that individual is in participating in the political process at more and more involved levels. One can think of these levels as concentric circles, going toward a center, from the least amount of involvement or level of participation at the first and largest circle to the highest level of participation at the center. The least amount of participation would be either nonparticipation or minimal participation, such as signing petitions. Perfunctory voting in one or the other election could be the next level of participation. Registering citizens and encouraging others to vote as well as voting oneself could be the next. Joining interest groups, campaigning for candidates would be the next level. After that could be working for political parties and then becoming a candidate oneself. Here, the level of candidacy could vary in increasing degrees from local to state to national, and then at the national level from House to Senate to presidential candidate. Of course, this level of involvement could also include accepting positions within administrations all the way up to cabinet secretary or Supreme Court justice. By definition not all citizens participate all the way to the highest level possible, but the point remains that the higher one's socialization, the more involved the level of one's participation will be.

Of course, among all kinds of participation, voting is the most visible form and also the most common, as millions of Americans engage in this form of participation several times a year at all levels of government. Let us turn to that discussion next.

CHAPTER 9

Electoral Politics, Electoral Systems, and the Electoral College

We concluded our discussion of participation with a reference to the most visible form of participation, voting. Elections are essential to the very notion of democracy, for democratic systems can miss quite a few things and still be called democratic, but without free elections and without the right of citizens to vote, no system can call itself democratic no matter what else it has to offer.

Elections are also at the heart of democratic politics because they are the only determinant of who occupies the top positions of power in a democracy. Since so much rides on elections, the politics surrounding elections are often fierce and unforgiving. This is the one arena where no prisoners are taken in the American political system.

Electoral politics center most fiercely at the national level around congressional elections, and in congressional elections around the elections for the House of Representatives. There is less of a power struggle—for that is what is meant by electoral politics—around the Senate elections, because Senate elections are determined by the Constitution to mean two senators per state get elected regardless of the size of the population of the state. This was what the Great Compromise was partly about. House elections, on the other hand, are determined by a numbers game that is often subject to great debate and controversy. We are talking, of course, about the census and its correlation with the elections for the House of Representatives.

According to the U.S. Constitution, a counting of the people of the United States for the purpose of representation must be done every ten years (Article I, section 2). This counting is referred to as the census, though the word does not occur in the

Constitution. The last such counting was done in the Spring of 2000, and the numbers counted became the basis for representation in the House of Representatives. The counting of citizens, though tallied nation-wide, is done state by state, as the representation in the House is by state, and within the states, by district. Each congressional district is to be of roughly equal size, and the size of districts today is about 650,000 people.

The politics of elections already starts with the census and the question of fair and accurate counting. Undercounts in one state or overcounts in another would tend to under- or over-emphasize the political importance of these states as it would give them either disproportionate representation and voice in the House or not enough. As if that is not enough, the counting itself is subject to great controversy. On the one hand, people are saying every person must be sought out and counted. On the other, people are saying that it is impossible to count every single person accurately and thus one must come to statistically acceptable estimates. The people who are saying that counts must be accurate, however, also question who could and could not be counted as, paradoxically, too accurate a count might disadvantage entrenched interests by creating new constituencies for their political opponents. On the other hand, the people who are saying statistical averages are also weary of the method if it shows numbers less than what they would have expected in their core constituencies.

Then there is the problem of the upper limit on seats in the House. The question of counting would be far less vexing if indeed more numbers of people counted would result in more seats in the House without penalizing other states, but the way the House of Representatives is structured, because of a law passed in 1929, its seats are limited to 435. Thus, any increase in the numbers of residents in one state, results in losses of seats in other states. The situation of the House turns out to be a mixture of musical chairs and zero-sum games.

Once counts are finished and the results certified, each state must engage in the task of redrawing of its congressional districts to accommodate the new reality of more or less, as the case may be, residents in that state. Few are in the happy position of staying the same for any length of time, though the midwestern states and some of the smaller and more remote states often benefit from this kind of constancy. Redrawing of district boundaries is called "redistricting," and redistricting carries the game of electoral politics one step further.

Redistricting is done by the state legislatures together with the state governors for the purpose of drawing boundaries for the congressional districts for the House of Representatives. The politics comes in when the majority party in the state legislature wants to draw things in such a way that voters of its own stripe would have the majority in as many districts as possible. This is done so as to guarantee victory for a maximum number of candidates of that same party in the national elections for the House of Representatives, since only one person can win in each district. This is how the state parties through their members in the state legislatures and the governor's offices try to help their national party gain victories in the House of Representatives. The more state parties can achieve drawing districts in such a way as to give their party faithful voters the edge, the more they can assure victory for their fellow party candidates for national office. Of course, none of this is 100 percent accurate, but in the trying, political parties have achieved great successes, or so at least they claim.

Sometimes in their zeal to carve out districts for themselves with a maximum number of party faithful in them, state politicians go overboard and draw districts with such obvious connection to party lines that their opponents challenge them in court. When districts are drawn for obvious political gain, that is called "gerrymandering," and gerrymandering is illegal. This extreme case of overzealousness on the part of politicians aside, once the districts are redrawn and certified by the governor of the state, the House of Representatives must reapportion its seats to reflect the new reality of the distribution of the population of the United States in the various states of the union.

Reapportionment refers to the dividing of the 435 seats of the House according to the new amounts of districts by state, based on the new census. In the 1990 census, California gained 7 more seats from its previous 45 to give it a total of 52 seats out of the 435 total in the House. In the 2000 census, California gained an additional seat for a total of 53 in the House. That is almost 12 percent of the House for one state alone, and although not all the representatives from California are from the same political party, they still all are Californians and will press the case for California, if it should come down to that, over that of Nevada or Hawaii or New York. This disproportionate amount of power for one state makes other states nervous and this is much of what the crux of politics is about in the House. Of course, California is not alone in this. All of the large states that also have a sizable immigration pattern pose the same kind of risk for the many other states who find themselves losing power in the House as a result.

Lastly, the numbers of congressional districts arrived at through the census and redistricting also play a role in the presidential elections, as those numbers form the basis for the formula that determines the numbers of electoral college votes each state gets. The higher the number of congressional districts, the higher the number of electoral college votes for that state, since that number is determined by adding up the number of districts with the number of senators per state, which is always a constant of two. For this reason California now has 55 electoral college votes, close to 11 percent of the entire college, and more than 20 percent of the number of electoral college votes a candidate needs to win the presidency (270, an absolute majority of the electoral college). This percentage is tremendous, considering that to make up for the loss of California, the other candidate must gather at least one other big state like Texas, Florida, or New York, and a whole host of smaller states with 3 or 4 electoral college votes here and there. The presidential election in 2000 was testimony to the painful reality of that fact.

Now that we have an understanding of the politics of elections, let us look at how we choose who wins and by what margins: the U.S. electoral system.

Electoral systems are ways by which we decide who wins. Historically, the United States has had a variety of such systems, starting all the way with the most difficult threshold, that of unanimity. Though unanimity was never a requirement for winning elective office, it was a system adopted by the states under the Articles of Confederation for their decision-making process in the Continental Congress. It still is a system adopted for petty juries in criminal trials in the United States. This is an extremely high threshold, as one voice of dissent has effective veto over the whole matter, and thus to require this system for elections would practically guarantee stalemates in countries as large as the United States with the variety and frequency of elections that they have. This system is, however, still used in the Vatican by the synod of bishops that choose the Pope. It is also adopted by the Security Council of the United Nations and by the Council of the European Union for certain of its decisions.

The next threshold is that of majority requirement. Majority requirements are intricately linked with the very notion of democracy. Democracy, we are often told, means "50 percent plus 1." However, in terms of choosing its elected representatives, the United States does not adopt this system anymore. It adopts the next lowest threshold, which is that of plurality. But before we talk about plurality, a word more about majorities. Majority decision-making is still the norm for elected democratic bodies such as legislatures. The Congress, in fact, makes all its decisions by majority of one kind or another. Depending on the gravity of the matter, Congress will vote by simple majority, absolute majority or by extraordinary majority of two-thirds. Simple majority is also called "relative majority." Relative majority is 50 percent plus 1 of all the votes cast by the members present. Absolute majority is 50 percent plus 1 of the votes of all the members, present or not. It is a much higher threshold, and is rarely used in legislatures. It is, however, used by the electoral college in the United States to determine the winner of the presidential election. Two-thirds majority is the kind of majority that the U.S. Constitution requires in the case of constitutional amendments and in the case of impeachments of U.S. presidents in the Senate.

Finally, the notion of plurality. Plurality is the lowest requirement for elections possible. There cannot be a threshold lower than that, so then the question is why is it chosen by democratic countries and in particular this democratic country to decide who occupies elected office? It is chosen because one tries to avoid multiple elections. In situations where there are more than two candidates running for office, if the threshold for electoral victory is not lowered to plurality, then the possibility of run-off or second round elections always exists, since it is quite possible that no candidate gets the majority straight away. In countries where there are already many elections, such as the United States due to the federal character of its political system, calling for more elections would have an adverse effect on the turnout of voters in all probability. For this reason, the threshold is lowered to accommodate both the lack of enthusiasm for more elections and the impossibility of limiting the number of candidates running for office. Plurality requires the winner only to get the most votes (i.e., one more vote than the next highest vote getter) in order to win.

Next in this discussion of numbers of votes required to win is the more complex matter of how the size of electoral districts is decided and how many elected officials go forward from each of these "districts." This is the discussion of single -member districts versus proportional representation, and the system of "winner-takes-all" that is prevalent in the electoral college system in the United States.

Generally, there are two ways of organizing the territory in order to have elections. One can either have the entire country as one electoral region and say "Here are 435 seats we need to fill" or one can divide the country into honeycombs of roughly equal size districts and say "only one person from each district goes forward." Of course, there are options in between, such as saying so many people from each state go forward without specifying districts within the state, but generally speaking these are the two options. Proportional representation generally encourages many more voices—and thus political parties—to try and capture political office. Thus, some say this system gives people a net increase in democracy. Others argue that the system of proportional representation increases instability and chaos, making governance and predictability more difficult. Those who say the latter, prefer single-member districts because in such a system only one person can win per district and thus naturally only two political parties are encouraged to battle for seats everywhere, as every additional party in the fray would reduce the chance of all to get elected. This "law" was worked out by a Belgian statistician and bears his name, the Duverger law.

The notion of winner-takes-all, is also related to the single-member district voting system, since only one member can in fact go forward from each district, but it is more connected to the electoral college system in the United States, where, with the exception of two states (Maine and Nebraska), all the other states give all the electoral college votes to the candidate who won the plurality of the vote. Winner-takes-all is an all or nothing system that has raised a lot of eyebrows lately, especially when elections in states are very, very close and the winning candidate wins by only a few hundred votes state wide. Getting all of that state's votes by barely making the threshold has been considered by many as unfair and perhaps even undemocratic.

Given the relevance of this discussion in an election year and the interest the drawn out campaign seasons of Republicans and Democrats have generated with the American public, it is perhaps appropriate that we elaborate on some of the features of the electoral process that Americans are and will be experiencing in 2008.

First, a word on primaries and caucuses, which are a peculiar feature of the American political system and its electoral politics. Democracies generally have two choices on how to thin the field of candidates to reach possible electoral victory for one. Either the field must be thinned before the general election occurs or there must be a first and a second round of general elections to determine the final victor. American national politics has opted to thin the field before the general election in part because in the American system voters are called upon to vote more than in other political systems, given that a federal structure creates one additional layer of government than the alternatives of unitary and confederate territorial division would. Another reason why Americans prefer to thin the field ahead of time rather than have two rounds of general elections is the psychological preference for closure that Americans have expressed over and over again. The proof of this was seen in the "indecision" of 2000 when Americans were faced with three painful months of waiting for an outcome of the Florida vote and thus of who had won the presidency.

Primaries and caucuses are different methods used to achieve the same end. Both are internal to the respective political parties, Democrat and Republican, and are organized nation-wide, by state, by the respective political parties, leading up to the national party conventions in late summer of the presidential election year. By state, primaries and caucuses can be open or closed, or, in the case of California in 2008, as if things are not complicated enough already, mixed. Open primaries allow registered voters to vote in the primaries of whichever party they wish to vote in. Closed primaries only allow voters who, when registering, indicated that party as their preferred party to vote in that party's primary. Mixed primaries, which California introduced in 2008, allowed independents (that is those who had indicated no particular party preference on their voter registration forms) to vote in the Democratic primary but did not allow any voters but registered Republicans to vote in the Republican primary. These decisions were made by the parties themselves based on their calculations as to what would get them maximum success in sifting through their fields of candidates and having the most viable of them emerge.

The prize for most bizarre and archaic system, though, must go to the Democratic primary/caucus system of Texas, the only state in the union to have a double system for the Democratic side, which in good Texas fashion is called the "Texas two-step." In this system, delegates are assigned through a primary formula that can baffle the hardiest of primary experts (proportional by district), and then, as if this was not complicated enough, final delegate counts are consolidated only when the primary voters come back for a caucus, thus the name "two-step." Former President Clinton remarked on this odd set-up in a stump speech for his wife ahead of the March 4, 2008, election in Texas, saying "Texas is the only state in the Union, where you can vote twice in the same election and not be arrested!" Indeed, this is what Democratic voters must do if they wish to have their say in the primary/caucus system of Texas. Of the 228 delegates at stake, 126 are tied to the primaries and 67 to the caucuses (with 12 superdelegates at stake as well that are not voted on). The 67 delegates at stake in the caucus can only be won if voters come back for the caucus after having voted in the primaries when the primary polls are closed. The results of the caucuses are then not announced until later that year, but those of the primaries are known immediately.

Primaries call upon registered voters to cast a vote for their preferred candidate from that party. For each state, the respective parties decide whether the winner of the primary will be chosen through the "winner-takes-all" method or that of "proportional representation." If winner takes all, then the entire delegate number for that state goes to the candidate with the most votes. If proportional representation, then the candidates get numbers of delegates based on the percentage of votes they have received state wide. To complicate matters further, Democrats in some states not only have proportional representation state wide, but assign districts on proportional representation as well. Republicans, as in all things, tend to eschew these complications and as a rule tend to prefer winner-takes-all. This allows them to find their frontrunner much more speedily than the Democrats, as witnessed by the length of time the Democrats needed to settle out their frontrunner in the Spring of 2008, Senator Barack Obama.

Caucuses are a more complicated affair, especially the version used by the Democratic party. For the Democratic caucus, registered Democrats gather at precincts and physically congregate in different corners for their preferred candidate. After attempting to persuade others to change their minds and join them in their corners instead, the precinct directors count the number of adherents for each candidate and the ones with 15 percent or more are declared winners in proportion to the number of people they had present and voting for them at that precinct. The numbers are then called in to a central location in each state and based on the grand total a winner for that state is declared. If the party had decided that that particular state was winner-takes-all, then one winner is declared and all the delegates for that state for that party are given to that frontrunner, if not, then the delegates for that state are apportioned to the various candidates based on the percentages of votes they have received in that state. Republican caucuses, again, are a simpler affair and resemble more primaries than caucuses. Republicans must physically show up for their caucuses but instead of "caucusing" they simply vote for their preferred candidate at those precincts and go home. The numbers are then called in to a central location by the directors and the winner for that state is declared that way, mostly on a winner-takes-all system, since as already discussed, Republicans prefer the closure this system provides.

At stake in each state are a number of delegates, based on a complicated formula, the total number of which varies for Democrats and Republicans. The number of delegates for each party in all fifty states, Washington, D.C., and dependent territories adds up to 4049 for the Democrats and 2380 for the Republicans. This is the total number of delegates that will gather at the respective party conventions in August of 2008, in Minneapolis and Denver. To win the nomination of their party, the Democratic and Republican candidates must gather an absolute majority of the delegates of their respective parties: 2025 for the Democrats and 1191 for the Republicans.

Matters are again complicated further a bit in that both the Republicans and the Democrats have two sets of delegates to their conventions: one set of state delegates called "pledged delegates," namely, the ones the candidates won through the caucus and primary systems in the respective states and which are "bound" to vote for the candidates who won those states. The other set are called "unpledged" or "superdelegates" (Republicans call theirs "unpledged" and

Democrats theirs "superdelegates"); they are not won through the election process and are not bound to vote in accord with the popular vote. The Democrats have 796 superdelegates and the Republicans 463 unpledged ones and these delegates are part of the total number of delegates for each party. All elected Democratic representatives in the House and Senate and Democratic governors and party officials make up the superdelegates of the Democrats. Of the 463 Republican ones, 123 are Republican National Committee (RNC) members, the rest are chosen by party officials. Both the unpledged and the superdelegates can, if they so choose, vote their "conscience" as opposed to how the voting populace has indicated. In that, they are very similar to the electors in the electoral college who can also vote their conscience, popular vote to the contrary not withstanding!

In 2008, an additional feature was added to the primary season: the dates of close to three-fourths of the primaries and caucuses (37 states in all) were moved up so that they were completed before the end of February. Never in the history of the United States was there a phenomenon similar to the new Super Tuesday (February 5) (quickly dubbed "Super Duper Tuesday") that was created as a result of this move, in which almost half the states of the union had their primaries and caucuses at once (24 states). Adding in Texas, Ohio, Rhode Island, and Vermont, whose primaries were on March 4, 2008, with only one important state left, Pennsylvania, whose primary was set for April 22, 2008. Given that the 2008 conventions of the Democratic and Republican parties were also set for August and September respectively, one can see on the one hand the trend to earlier primaries and caucuses to be kingmakers on the front end and to later and later party conventions closer to the general election so as to carry maximum momentum in the collective memory of Americans come general election day, November 4, 2008.

Primaries and caucuses are peculiar to the American political process as preliminary elections before the general election, yet they are not the only elections that are peculiar to the American system. Uniquely, in the American system, the president is elected indirectly, first by popular vote in the general election, but then through a vote by the electoral college, six weeks after the general election. (While the general election is held by law on the first Tuesday after the first Monday in November, the electors of the electoral college meet in their respective state capitals and in Washington, D.C., on the first Monday after the second Wednesday in December, and cast their ballots separately for president and vice-president.) It is this second vote, the electoral college vote, that determines who is president of the United States. The popular vote does not. Immediately, of course, students ask whether the popular vote matters at all then since the electoral college vote is the determining vote after all. The answer is that the popular vote matters, of course, it is just that it is does not matter with finality. But before we move on, it is perhaps appropriate that we elaborate on the electoral college a bit.

The electoral college is a collection of electors chosen by state, totaling 538. This number is arrived at by adding up the number of House seats per state and the number of Senate seats per state (a constant two). In addition, three electors are added for Washington, D.C., a peculiarity again, since Washington, D.C., is not a state and thus deprived of the privilege of electing any United States representatives at all except for participating in the presidential election. The total number of seats in the House of Representatives is 435. The total number of senators in the Senate is 100 (given 50 states in the Union at present). These numbers plus the three electors from Washington, D.C., make up the total of 538 for the electoral college.

Each state is thus entitled to a fixed number of electors, the number of which is determined with each census since part of the formula that determines this number is based on the number of House seats the state has, and the number of House seats is of course based on the population of that state which is determined in turn by the census every ten years (a.k.a. the decennial census). Before the general election, each state party chooses a slate of electors equal to the total number of electors allotted to that state in order to prepare for the eventuality of the popular vote going their candidate's way. This is why the popular vote *does* matter since the popular vote determines which slate of electors remains and which slates are dismissed. It is true that electors need not vote the way the popular vote in that state indicated, but the initial choice of which slate of electors remains does follow the popular vote and is determined by it. Thus if we were to take the example of California in the 2004 presidential election, California was allotted 55 electors as a result of the 2000 census. The California Republican and Democratic parties chose 55 electors, respectively, in 2004. These slates of electors waited for the results of the popular vote in 2004. In 2004, California's popular vote went for Senator Kerry over President Bush, thus the 55 Democratic electors remained and the Republican slate was dismissed. These 55 Democratic electors then cast their ballots for Senator Kerry and Senator Edwards for president and vice-president, respectively, in Sacramento in the second week in December 2004. Their counterparts in 49 other states and in the District of Columbia did the same thing and the outcome was that President George Bush was re-elected and Senator Kerry lost despite the fact that he had carried the biggest prize, California.

To be declared president-elect (the official title of the winner of the electoral college vote until he/she has taken the oath of office on January 20 of the next year), a person must have gotten at least 270 of the 538 electoral college votes, an absolute majority of the electoral college votes. Given this requirement, it becomes clear why California is the biggest prize of all, since, as stated earlier already, California by itself has more than 20 percent of the votes required to win the absolute majority of the electoral college vote, Texas, Florida, New York, and Illinois being states with large numbers of electors also. Given the special position of California both as the largest electoral college state and a traditionally Democratic state in the presidential race, California Republicans attempted to introduce a state ballot measure for the June 2008 ballot in California that would change the way California's 55 electoral college votes are apportioned from winner-takes-all to proportional representation. The thinking was that since Republicans have a majority in 19 of the 53 Congressional Districts in California, they could manage to have at least 19 of the electoral college votes of the state with this new system rather than none under the current winner-takes-all regime. This maneuver generated huge opposition and cries of foul play by Democrats, who argued that this was a blatant attempt to influence the upcoming 2008 election in the direction of the Republicans and that if any changes were made they should be made in Texas and Florida and other large states as well, states the Republicans did not want to see tinkered with since they had advantages there. The effort bore no fruit, however, since the backers of the effort ran out of funds and support before the signature-gathering deadline of November 2007, but it introduced a new and interesting dimension into the electoral college debate that will surely resurface in one form or another soon again.

Part III:
Institutions

CHAPTER 10

Interest Groups and Political Parties

Interest groups and political parties are the two most prominent institutions within the political system to link the people (citizens) with government, and thus allow the citizenry to attempt to influence the outcome of the political system. For this reason, interest groups and political parties are referred to as linkage institutions. In a pluralist system like that of the United States, linkage institutions are crucial in connecting people with the system, since most of the day-to-day interaction between people and the political system occurs through the medium of these institutions.

We have talked about the role of interest groups and that of political parties briefly in the lecture on the model of the political system. We have also explored the role of interest groups in shaping the nature of pluralism in America in the lecture on models of democracy. Here, we will briefly explore their role as linkage institutions and the functions they perform as a result of that role.

Interest groups are uniquely positioned in the American political system in that they are in fact the main link between people and the political system, outside the exceptional moments when individuals vote for their representatives or when they take large scale action to influence their representatives through marches or demonstrations or letter-writing campaigns and petitions. Because of the nature of the American political system, as described in the discussion on pluralism and hyperpluralism in chapter 2, interest groups are not only links to the political system that dispassionately relate issues raised by the people to the various institutions in the system but they also become gatekeepers to the system by the fact that they are the arbiters of what goes in and what does not due to their prominence and size, and due to the fact that most people cannot or do not interact with the system on a day-to-day basis in any other way. This is what was meant by the discussion of hyperpluralism as an "undermining of the very notion of pluralism, and not just being another version of it."

The traditional notion of the role of interest groups in the political system is that of "interest articulation." Indeed, this is one of the things interest groups do. They amplify and clarify issues raised by the people and bring them into the political system for the other institutions in the system to pick up and act upon, ultimately turning those issues into policy. One of the main ways by which interest groups achieve this is through their connection with the political parties in the system. Interest groups bring their issues to the parties, who in turn incorporate them into their platforms as "planks." (More on this below.) But this is not the only thing interest groups do within the system. Interest groups do not just passively wait their turn after having passed on the issue to political parties. Interest groups actively seek to advance their agendas by a variety of means, one of which is to ensure that their issue gets on the platform of this or that political party. The other actions interest groups take to further their agendas have been discussed under the rubric of "Interest Group Strategies" by Lowi, Ginsberg, and Weir in their book *We the People* (2007). Chiefly, these strategies include lobbying. Lobbying can be defined as singling out key individuals, mainly in the legislature, and pressing one's case with them in order to achieve the desired ends. Of course, this is not as simple a task as presenting one's case and hoping for the best. Interest groups have a variety of means at their disposal to make their case forcefully with those key individuals in the system, chief among them being the monetary clout that many of these groups can wield.

Legislators depend on large sums of money in order to be able to run successful campaigns. Much of the monies raised by legislators, and politicians in general, come from donations by interest groups through Political Action Committee, or PAC, money. PAC donations to politicians have approached the billion dollar mark in recent years, and the strongest of these interest groups have been able to donate the kinds of sums of money that could make a difference in the election chances of their chosen candidate. As a result, these groups particularly have access to the politicians to whom they contributed vitally. This is what hyperpluralism represents. Stronger and well-endowed groups have privileged access as a result of their monetary clout.

In its most recent attempt to curb the flow of money to politicians, Congress passed the McCain-Feingold Campaign Finance Reform Act of 2002, also known as the Bipartisan Campaign Reform Act of 2002 (BCRA) on account of the joint sponsorship of the Act by Republican Senator John McCain (yes, the self-same McCain who is now in 2008 the Republican candidate for the presidency of the United States and whom his fellow Republicans and conservatives have not forgiven for the work he did among other things on this very bill) and Democrat Russ Feingold. The McCain-Feingold Act, not unlike the Federal Election Campaign Act (FECA) of 1975 that brought about the Federal Election Commission (FEC), whose charge is campaign finance monitoring and regulation, was meant to limit the flow of money in politics by making it harder for interest groups and individuals to funnel monies to politicians.

Just as in 1975, so also in 2002, rather than stemming the flow of money, the act opened other avenues for campaign finance such as the creation of the 527 nonprofit organizations, so named after the section of the law that addresses their creation and legal status, that made some lobbyists exclaim gleefully, "it is business as usual, only better." Indeed, the 527s have allowed people to donate unlimited amounts of money to political causes without having to disclose the origin of the donors as long as the monies are used for so called "issue ads." It was this loophole in the law that gave us new political categories such as "swift-boating," in reference to the ads running during the 2004 presidential campaign, purportedly by swift boat veterans of the Vietnam War, smearing the military record of Democratic presidential candidate Senator John Kerry, by claiming that he abandoned his platoon and he caused the deaths of Vietnamese civilians and that some of his wounds were self-inflicted to gain the purple stars he received. The creation of 527s has meant an exponential increase in the flow of money in politics by interest groups in contravention of the very spirit of the McCain-Feingold law that was responsible for their coming into existence in the first place.

Interest groups also use other means by which they get their special issues across. One of the more prominent ways by which they can assure that their voice is heard is the ability to influence courts through what are called "friends of the court" or *amicus curiae* legal briefs detailing the merits of their case, or by outright suing in the courts to get their way with weaker adversaries who may not be able to afford prolonged legal battles. Another more nefarious way still for interest groups to get their way in the system is to form what political scientists have called "iron triangles." Iron triangles are close-knit connections that become almost permanent in nature, among legislators, the special interest groups and the bureaucracy in charge of either regulating that industry or implementing that policy. What these iron triangles achieve is to make access to politicians by other groups and the people at large very difficult if not impossible. Again power begets more power, and interest groups with that kind of clout have practically no viable opponents in the system, and can get their pet issues through almost unimpeded. There would be no problem with this except for the fact that these arrangements keep out everybody else except the one group that has a lock on the system. This fact contradicts the very notion of pluralism and democracy, but is not uncommon in the American system. Some of the most notorious iron triangles are those of the defense industry, something President Eisenhower called the "military-industrial complex."

Political parties, the other main linkage institution, also do more than simply gather issues brought to their attention by the interest groups. We argued in the lecture on the model of the political system, that they aggregated issues, and indeed they do that. The physical manifestation of that aggregation is the platform of each of these political parties. We have also said that they socialize individuals on behalf of the system by educating them on the issues and giving that education an ideological framework. We have also argued that they recruit on behalf of the system. And, indeed, this is perhaps the most prominent aspect of political parties in the political system, the other functions just described aside.

Political parties are the main recruiters of politicians into the system. Without political party support no politician can hope to win national office in the system today, though there have been one or two exceptions to this in recent years, most notably presidential candidate Ross Perot and most recently Senator Joseph Liebermann who was re-elected as an independent. Political parties also, through their quadrennial conventions become the main kingmakers for the presidential campaign in the American political system. Their support is crucial for anyone seeking the highest office of the land, and thus political parties, too, become gate-keepers and not just conveyors of issues.

Political parties also become more than bridges between the people and the system in another way. Since political parties anoint and support candidates, candidates who receive the kind of support political parties offer become beholden to the party once elected. What that means in practice is that once the candidate is elected to office, they take with them the platform of that party into office and are expected to act on that platform and the issues it includes by proposing and supporting legislation to that effect. How parties ensure that this will in fact happen is explained by the notions of "party outside government" and "party inside government."

"Party outside government" refers to the organization of the party inside the political system and in society at large that allows the party to raise funds, have a membership and a full-time leadership at the national, state and local levels, create platforms, anoint candidates and have conventions. "Party inside government" refers to the organization inside the legislature of the candidates along party lines. This is where the notion of congressional leadership comes in. The leaders of the House of Representatives and the Senate are not only occupying their positions of Speaker or President pro-tem as part of their elected office, these leaders also are leaders of their respective political parties inside Congress. The main task of the leadership inside Congress is to see to it that its party's agenda is passed into law. This agenda is, of course, composed of the very issues that the interest groups successfully managed to place on the platform of these parties and that the lobbyists successfully pressed for after key candidates they supported in tandem with the parties made it into political office.

This is how the circle of influence and power is closed, and this is also how interest groups and political parties in the American context become more than simple automatons on a conveyer belt passing on to the next level what had previously been passed on to them. As a result of this complex interaction, it is only natural that parties and interest groups end up doing more than what one would expect of them at first glance, in view of the fact that so much rides on the victory of one issue over another. But as with everything else in democracy, so also with this. Issues are only settled for a day, if that. The next day, as soon as a law is passed and a policy is decided upon, the battle begins anew. A battle either for the repeal of the bill just passed, or a battle to introduce further legislation to strengthen it. Such is the nature of democracy that nothing, nothing, is ever settled for long.

Having looked at the electoral system and interest groups and political parties and their functions, it is proper now to look at the institutions of government. The electoral process leads to the choice of occupants for these institutions; the pressure by interest groups and political parties results in the kind of policies these institutions will espouse and the decisions they will come to make. Let us look at the first of these institutions now, the Congress.

CHAPTER 11

Congress: The Legislative Branch

Congress is the first branch of the U.S. government. Every student of the U.S. Constitution and every student of American government has heard this statement and reflected upon its meaning. Indeed, in the Constitution, Congress is dealt with at length and first, above, beyond, and before the other two branches. Congress is endowed with enormous powers, hardly captured by the phrases "All legislative powers herein granted shall be vested in a Congress of the United States," and "Congress shall have power to make all laws, which shall be necessary and proper."

Even a cursory, comparative glance at the founding articles of the three branches of the U.S. government, Articles I, II, and III of the U.S. Constitution, already tells a convincing story. Article I, dealing with Congress, is two and a half times as long as Article II, which deals with the powers of the president, and three times as long as Article III, which deals with the U.S. Supreme Court. Needless to say, this disparity is not due to a dwindling creative outburst by the framers, which progressively atrophies as the articles increase in number. The disparity has to do with substance, and substance in the U.S. Constitution has to do with power.

Sections 7 and 8 of Article I of the Constitution paint a picture of a Congress that is at the helm of the government of the United States in all its vital functions. Congress, of course, has the power to "make all laws." From this power flows the work of government. Without laws, no action of government is possible or legitimate. Yes, Congress must cooperate with the president in trying to get its bills promulgated into law, but it has the power to overcome presidential disapproval if the situation requires it. The reverse is not true.

Section 8 completes and rounds off the picture of the extent of Congress' powers. While covering all aspects of day-to-day governance, of the eighteen clauses of this section, eight (including clause 17 dealing with sovereignty over the District of Columbia), are dedicated to matters students of government usually associate with the executive branch, namely, the wherewithal of war making and defense. Seven clauses deal with economic matters properly thought of as powers of the purse and traditionally given to the legislative branch. One clause, clause 9, deals with the very capacity of the judicial branch to operate, a point repeated again in

Article III, section 1. And, finally, clause 18, the elastic or "necessary and proper" change, tells us that if anything was forgotten in the above seventeen, Congress has the power to do that as well. But what of the much celebrated powers of the President of the United States?

A closer look at the letter of Article II of the Constitution reveals that on almost every aspect of the president's power that matters, there is, if not a say so by Congress as a whole, at least the say so of one of its chambers, the Senate. This is true even of the most celebrated power of the president, that of being commander-in-chief, even though in practice this has been mitigated by the War Powers Act of 1973. The phrase "the President proposes and Congress disposes" best captures the situation related in Article II, section 2, regarding the President's ability to legally bind the country to courses of action Congress disapproves of. This is also true of the president's ability to choose his own cabinet with finality, or to decide who serves on the highest bench of the land. And, of course, Congress can remove and try the president for "high crimes and misdemeanors," a phrase the full impact of which may not soon be forgotten, even by a generation whose attention span is dictated by sound bites and mega bites, given the historic impeachment proceedings of 1998 against President Clinton.

All this Congress is endowed with according to the Constitution, and yet there is more to this notion of Congress being the first branch than a simple listing of its powers compared to those of the president or the Supreme Court could reveal. What makes Congress the first branch comes to light in the daily practice of the American political system, which goes far beyond the letter of the Constitution, even though this practice of governing America finds its roots and legitimization in the very words of the Constitution.

In the American political system, as in every other democratic political system, the legislative branch is the first branch in which the policy-making process begins. Laws are at the origin of the legitimate game of policy-making in the political system, and Congress is where the laws in America are made. Thus Congress and the representatives therein become the focus and the first step in the elaborate dance that is the dance of legislation, promulgation and implementation, in short, of policy-making, that is the raison d'être of the entire political system in America.

In this elaborate dance, the role of Congress is paramount, because without Congress' willingness to take the first step, the dance itself cannot begin. Two examples should make this point clear. The first is the mandate in Article I, section 7, that all revenue bills must originate in the House of Representatives. Taken at face value, this mandate simply means that the Senate may not initiate such bills, and thus it could be read as a tilt by the Founding Fathers toward the House, since in it are found representatives who are closer to the people of the United States, in every way, than are their more imperious peers in the Senate. But on closer scrutiny, this little phrase also acknowledges that unless Congress, in this case specifically the House, so wishes, there is no revenue bill to speak of, and thus no possibility of raising funds or expending them, and thus really no blood to course in the veins of government. This is a powerful reminder of where the dance begins.

The other example, underlining the necessity of Congress to initiate the first step without which there is no dance, is, of course, the memorable one of a few years ago, when the new Republican majority in Congress, elected through the strategy of the *Contract with America*, wanted to flex its newly acquired legislative muscle. It decided to stall all decisions the president was eagerly awaiting on the budget, to the point that the entire government came to a complete shut down. True, in the end, it was the Republicans who lost that gamble in the eyes of the American people, and ultimately their maverick leader, Newt Gingrich, was made to pay for his hubris by having to resign his position of Speaker of the House. True also that it was the president who by exercising one of his few real powers, made Congress stay in Washington beyond their recess date until they had hammered out a budget with him. The point, however, remains, that without Congress' willingness to take the first step, the entire political system comes to a halt. A president's unwillingness to act, though troublesome, can ultimately be overcome by a simple act of Congress. The reverse is not true. That is a true proof of power. A power found nowhere else in the American political system. It can be argued that the Budget and Impoundment Control Act of 1974, passed by Congress in response to President Nixon's attempts to impede Congress from spending monies it had already appropriated, conclusively settled this particular question of who can stop whose work with finality. Of course, in the above example Congress gave in and not the president, but the crisis was only resolved because it lost the battle in the media, not because the president had constitutional tools at his disposal that would allow him to override Congress' will.

Being that Congress is so powerful, and being that America is a democracy, there ought to, therefore, be cause for celebration by the American people, that they are the proven masters of their political fortunes. Yet when probed on the question of how they feel about their political system and their say in it, Americans almost always express a feeling of helplessness regarding their institutions, particularly Congress, and often perceive themselves as subjects not masters of their own political destiny. Should Americans feel this way? Of course not. America is a democracy, and democracy means that the people govern. Why do Americans feel this way then? The answer to this question is twofold: the first part has to do with the kind of democracy America is. The second, and more troublesome part, has to do with the kind of democracy America has become. The first is by design. The second, one would have to hope, by default, and this is where the notion of reform of the system legitimately enters the arena.

The American political system involves its citizens primarily by devolving upon them the burden of choosing their representatives. Beyond that choice and thereafter, Americans as a whole are barely involved in the political system directly, and power of decision-making naturally falls upon the representatives and not upon the citizens in America. This fact is encapsulated in the very notion of representative democracy, of course, but in the United States it goes far beyond that, in that the system itself makes involvement by the citizen qua citizen redundant and often very difficult.

Majoritarianism, with all its implications of mass public involvement in the decision-making process and the possible raising of the specter of direct democracy is as far from American political practice as democracy would allow. Shays' Rebellion and perhaps also the action of the mobs in France at the time of the French Revolution, taught that lesson to the Founding Fathers early and well. For these reasons, the people are present through their representatives in the American political system. People are decision-makers only in the remotest sense of the word when it comes to day-to-day politics in America. In envisioning this process, James Madison, in Federalist No.10, speaks of the virtue of competition of interests in a republic through the representative process over that of direct involvement of the citizen, and chooses carefully to outline the virtues of this form of government over that which he calls a "democracy," and by which he means Rousseau's version of things. (See Madison's Federalist No. 10 in Appendix C.)

Not being present in large numbers on a daily basis does not mean, however, that the American people find no access to their elected representatives beyond the ballot box; quite to the contrary. In the daily practice of politics in America, citizens find access to their representatives mostly through an elaborate filtration device called the interest group system, leading to what Theodore Lowi, one of the more prominent contemporary political scientists, has called "interest-group liberalism," the predominance of interest groups in the American political system competing for and capturing the attention of the representatives. Taken at face value, this system, though somewhat different from that envisioned by Madison, still does not present evident problems, as nothing in the laws or the practice of the American system bars citizens from reaching their representatives on an individual basis, or in a variety of other ways, some specifically protected by the First Amendment to the Constitution. And, of course, there is always the ballot box and the next election in which to express one's opinion by either "throwing out the bums," or reelecting one's favorite candidate.

Interest groups as representatives of the voices of the people—albeit of the voice of a far smaller segment than the population at large—direct the energies of the American political system to the legislature as the first step toward the realization of the aim of the political game, namely, the successful passage of legislation in one's own favor. However, interest groups, more and more, have had to carve out access to the system, and to Congress in particular, at higher and higher costs. As politics and politicking has gotten more expensive (FEC figures for the 2006–7 campaign put expenditures by PACs at close to one billion dollars), so has access to politicians. When, some years ago now, Senator Paul Simon of Illinois decided not to run for reelection, he cited the burden of fundraising as one of the main reasons for not wanting to stay in anymore. Since money has become the dominant issue in politics, only those with money can guarantee themselves access. Everyone else has to wait in line and wait their turn. This development has been called hyperpluralism by Robert Lineberry and his colleagues, a process that twists the logic of representation through interest groups, still further, by producing two new realities. One is the proliferation of interest groups vying for the attention of the legislators who have developed an almost exclusive ear for their way of petitioning them. Two is a crowding out of smaller (i.e., less endowed) groups by larger well-endowed groups who can foot the bill representatives need in order to run meaningful reelection campaigns.

If we are correct in our earlier assertion that Congress is the most powerful branch of government in the United States; and if we are correct in our assertion that the Founding Fathers set Congress up as such because of their particular vision of what this political system should be; and if we are also correct that this body has shifted further and further away from the people through a logic only partly created by itself, then we must, of course, argue that the system needs change in order to legitimately retain its appellation of representative democracy, and the developments we have traced here are to be viewed with utmost concern.

Let us now look at the role the president has to play in the dance of legislation under the doctrine of checks and balances in the American political system.

CHAPTER 12

Legislative Role of President (As per Article 1.7 and Congressional Law)

The form of government of the United States is called a presidential form of government (see Chapter 4 on presidential versus parliamentary form of government). What this implies among other things is that there is a strict separation of power between the executive and legislative branches. But the architects of the American political system and the balance of power that goes with it, also saw the necessity of linking these two branches now that they had been separated for the sake of better governance. This re-linking of the legislative and executive (and the judiciary, also) is called checks and balances, and has been addressed in Chapter 7 at greater length. In this context here, the context of the legislative role of the president, the idea of checks and balances comes especially to life.

According to the architects of the U.S. Constitution, no bill can become law until it has *first* been presented to the president, who then will have several options as to his response to that bill. The idea—and this is important—is *not* that the president has *final say* over whether a bill becomes law or not—that would be akin to absolutism—but that *Congress* does not have final say over whether a bill becomes law, because that would be "legislative tyranny." To build in a legislative role for the president was a signal to Congress, just as including an executive role for the Senate, and for Congress in general, was a signal to the president that he is not the sole governor of the land.

Of course bills need not be signed by the president for them to become law, nor does the law of the land need to have been passed by Congress for it to be the law of the land (see below for explanation on how this is so). The idea is one of cooperation between the two branches, and this cooperation is laid out in the steps listed below as outlined in Article I, section 7, of the U.S. Constitution.

A bill, before it is presented to the president, must be passed by both the House and the Senate (see remarks on bicameralism in Chapter 7). When this has occurred, the president has two choices as per Article I, section 7, of the U.S. Constitution: He can say YES or can say NO to the bill. If he says "YES," then he signs the bill and it becomes *law*, a process usually concluded with great fanfare in Rose Garden ceremonies at the White House if the bill is an important one for the president and his supporters. If he says "NO," however, then the president can do one of *three* things: The president can:

1. VETO the bill and send it back to that "house" (chamber) of Congress from which it originated, together with his objections. That "house" then, can reconsider the bill and either agree with the president's objections or vote by 2/3 to "override" the president's veto. Then the same must be done by the other "house." If they both override by a 2/3 majority, then the bill becomes law over the objection(s) of the president. (The override is final. The president has no more say on that law.)

2. DO NOTHING and let the bill sit on his desk for ten days ("Sundays excepted"). The bill becomes law without the president's signature. (Presidents do this when they do not have assurance that their veto will stick but still want to show the people that the bill is not a good one in their judgment.)

3. POCKET VETO and the bill sits on the desk of the president for ten days ("Sundays excepted") and Congress goes into recess within those ten days. The bill cannot be returned to Congress. The bill dies. No resuscitation is possible. Legislators must start all over if they want legislation to that effect.

A fourth option existed until 1996, the LINE-ITEM VETO. By congressional law, the president could "veto" parts of a bill (budget, for instance) while retaining the remainder. He could do so by "crossing out" (drawing a line) on the undesirable part(s) of the bill. Congress (both houses) could then re-institute those parts by a majority vote in each house, which then, in turn, would be subject again to a presidential veto, which then would be subject to an override by Congress. Failing that override by a two-thirds majority in both houses the line-item veto would stick.

This last power of the line-item veto was a "constitutionally dubious" power. From the get-go, when Congress passed the Line-Item Veto Act into law in April of 1996 and when it became effective on January 1, 1997, it was highly questionable whether or not the Supreme Court would agree with this expansion of presidential power as conforming to the U.S. Constitution. In fact, the Supreme Court had already had an opportunity to decide on the matter in June of 1997, in the case of *Raines v. Byrd et al* (USSC 96-1671). Unfortunately, the decision of the Supreme Court in 1997 was not one on the substance of this new power but rather on the "standing" of those who sued to bring this case before the Court. In its response, the Court argued then that since the president had not used the power yet there was no ground to sue. Later that year, the president did use his newly acquired power to line-item veto (on August 11, 1997) some provisions of the budget bill given to him by Congress, and the debate re-opened.

There was never a question in the minds of many observers that this new power was a violation of the Constitution's spirit and letter regarding both the limits it set on presidential power and on the process it set up for changes (amendments) that are intended for its provisions. The Founding Fathers clearly wanted the president to have to say yes or no to an *entire* bill and not to pieces of it, *and* they wanted changes to what they had written into the Constitution to be made with utmost deliberation and difficulty (by a vote of 2/3 of both houses *and* 3/4 of the state legislatures [Article V], for instance). This new power failed both those tests. In June of 1998, in the case of *William Jefferson Clinton v. City of New York* (USSC 97-1374), the line-item veto power was indeed declared unconstitutional and is thus no more part of the legislative powers of the president.

There is, however, another "legislative power" that the president possesses that is not referred to in Article I, section 7, and for that matter not even referred to in the letter of the Constitution. That power is the president's power to issue executive orders that have the force of law. This power was given to the president by the Supreme Court in the case of *In re Neagle* (1890), where the Court argued that the president, in pursuance to his mandate to see to it that "the laws be faithfully executed" (U.S. Constitution, Article II, section 3), could mandate government agencies to carry out his orders, which orders would have the force of law.

In an interesting twist of events, in the first week of March 2001, Congress took it upon itself, based upon a Congressional Act of 1996, to annul such acts of the president, which it found onerous, by a simple majority vote in both houses. The order Congress thus annulled was the order given by President Clinton in 2000 that mandated businesses to see to it that workers were not subject to repetitive motion syndrome. Business howled at this order from the start. When Congress saw the opportunity to assert its power over the presidency, it took that opportunity and undid what it always saw as an unwarranted assertion of presidential prerogative on its legislative turf. That the Republican Congress set a dangerous precedent here should be obvious, because Republicans will not always last in the White House and in Congress simultaneously, and when that shoe will be on the other foot, Democrats surely will seize the opportunity to return the favor in time. Congress, after having tasted blood on this executive order, looked at another provision President Clinton issued an executive order for before leaving office, the blocking of access road building on millions of federally owned acres of timberland. President Bush put a hundred-day moratorium on the order in the first days of his taking office in January 2001 and Congress proposed to undo this Clinton order as well by the same means it undid the previous one.

Next we turn to a further consideration of the powers of the presidency.

CHAPTER 13

The Presidency

In comparison to the legislative, the executive branch was designed by the Founding Fathers to be a caretaker rather than a leader. There is one obvious reference to "leadership" in Article II of the Constitution and that is in reference to the "power" of the president to be "commander-in-chief" when a war is declared and an army has been raised and paid for by Congress. The fact that the presidency has become powerful today has little to do with the original design of the Constitution. It has much more to do with the development of the office over time, and even more so with the advent of military technology and the means of modern warfare and communication that have put the president in charge of a permanent armed force armed with nuclear missiles.

Below we want to look at the qualifications for office of the president as well as the actual powers of the president according to the Constitution and according to practice over the years. The result will be a realization that the president has more duties than powers, but that the few powers he has can be and have been used spectacularly to make him the most powerful head of state on the globe.

First, let us look at the requirements and qualifications for holding office. In order to become president, a candidate must satisfy the following requirements and qualifications, not more, not less! As per Article II, section 1, of the Constitution, the future president must be a natural born citizen, with a minimum of thirty-five years of age. He must have been a resident of the United States for at least fourteen years, and have no criminal record and certainly not be a felon or traitor to the United States at the time he proposes to run for office and be elected. The later provision is not given in Article II, section 1, but is assumed. On the question of treason, however, the Fourteenth Amendment states that such "disability" could be removed by Congress by a two-thirds vote by both houses, a clear reference to the Civil War and its aftermath. As to the likelihood of such a "disability" to be overlooked by the people or by the opponents of such candidate, we will leave that to the imagination of the reader.

In order to be elected, the future president must receive the plurality of the popular vote by state *and* receive the absolute majority of the electoral college vote (270 votes at present), according to the Twelfth Amendment to the Constitution. If such is the case, the person then is referred to as "President-Elect" until such time as he has taken the oath of office on January 20 following his election, as per Article II, section 1, of the Constitution. The oath of office, incidentally, does not include the words, "So help me God!" They were added to the oath by President George Washington at his first inaugural and were retained ever since by tradition, but could be argued to be repugnant to the spirit of the Constitution, and certainly are to the letter thereof. But no president who would not utter them on these grounds would stand a chance of reelection, and thus the question of the appropriateness of these words has never been raised, despite the fact that the Constitution explicitly states that "no religious test shall be required as a qualification to any office or public trust under the United States" (Article VI, paragraph 3).

The powers and duties of the president are described in Article II, sections 2 and 3, of the Constitution. What the student will note right away is that there are so many more duties to the office than there are powers, and that is not by default but rather by design. The Founding Fathers did not want the president to be an all-powerful king. They wanted him to be the first servant of the Republic, carrying out the will of the people as expressed through their representatives in Congress. They also did not, however, want him to be a servant to Congress, and so they did endow this president with certain powers with regard to Congress. In comparison to the powers of Congress over the president, however, the president definitely does not come out the winner.

First and foremost, the president has the power of the veto (Article I, section 7). This power has already been described in detail in the discussion on the legislative powers of the president, above. Next, the president is given the power of being "Commander-in-chief" of the armed forces. This power, however, is immediately curtailed in the wording of the Constitution by the phrase "when called into actual service of the U.S." (Article II, section 2). This phrase may not have much meaning today as the president is commander-in-chief over a standing, peace time, armed force that is in a constant state of readiness and does not need to be "called into actual service" by Congress. But when this power was originally granted, that was exactly the intention. An even cursory reading of the provisions of Article I, section 8, regarding the military powers of Congress should not leave any further doubt in this matter.

Another aspect of this power is also the fact that the president is the commander-in-chief over the nuclear arsenal of the United States. This also is an unforeseen development that propels the president to the forefront of the national government with the kind of power that is unmatched by any of the other branches of government. This, too, is not an intended development from the designs of the Founding Fathers but rather a technological imperative that has become the most awesome aspect of the power of the president.

Among the presidential powers that could be considered "absolute" is that of granting pardons. The only limitation that the president has in this regard is that he cannot grant pardons in cases of impeachment (Article II, section 2). This puts in perspective the canard that ran the rumor mill in Washington, D.C., in the fall of 1998, fanned by Representative Tom Campbell from California, among others, that the president could pardon himself in case he was impeached. This power has, however, often received unsought attention because of the high profile of the cases to which it was applied. President Ford, for instance, pardoned President Nixon to stop all further inquiries into his dealings in the Watergate affair. President Bush pardoned Secretary Caspar Weinberger in the Iran-Contra affair to stop any further proceedings against him and other defendants in that particular case, and, of course, President Clinton most recently used that power to pardon all kinds of people that later revealed themselves to be less than likeable characters, and these pardons have even raised the specter of Congress looking into curbing the power of pardon which it sees, and rightly we might add, as a last vestige from the monarchical tradition of England.

This power aside, which indeed is absolute in the sense that there is no further say-so on it by anyone else, the president further has the power to convene and adjourn both houses of Congress at his discretion. He can convene them "under extraordinary occasions" says the Constitution, and he can adjourn them "to such times as he shall think proper" (Article II, section 3). President Clinton used this power deftly in his dealings with the newly elected Republican Congress in 1995, by keeping Congress in session until they voted on his budget proposals, to the great astonishment and fury of the Republicans in Congress who wanted to go home for the Christmas holiday.

The president only has one more power to speak of and that is the power to fill vacancies that may happen during the recess of the Senate, "by granting commissions, which shall expire at the end of their next session." Again, President Clinton used this power to appoint an ambassador during the recess of the Senate, whose credentials had been rejected by the Senate through the insistence of then Senator Ashcroft (attorney-general of President Bush in the 2001–4 term), who objected to the nominee on grounds, say his opponents, that had nothing to do with the nominee's credentials and more with his sexual orientation of which Ashcroft, who is a conservative Christian, disapproved. This power, too, except for extraordinary cases, does not get much limelight in normal times. It was, however, used again and equally controversially by President Bush to appoint John Bolton as UN Ambassador in a recess appointment in June of 2005 over Democratic objections.

The remaining clauses and sections of Article II of the Constitution, dealing with the executive power, are not really lists of powers but rather duties of the president. They include the power to "make treaties" but "with the advice and consent of Senate," subject to a two-thirds ratification by the Senate of any treaty so signed by the president (Article II, section 2). The president further has the power to "nominate" individuals he wishes to have serve in his cabinet or on the federal bench. Again, this power is subject to the "advice and consent of the Senate," where a majority of the full Senate gets to confirm the presidential choice after that nominee has passed the sometimes grueling task of going through congressional confirmation hearings before the appropriate Senate committees (Article II, section 2).

The president further is mandated by the Constitution to give a yearly "State of the Union address" and make recommendations to Congress (Article II, section 3).

He is also mandated by Congress to give to it an economic report and a budget report on a yearly basis. This is not required by the Constitution but mandated by Congress and abided by the president. The president is also empowered to receive foreign dignitaries and, lastly, is mandated to "take care that the laws be faithfully executed" (Article II, section 3). President Clinton was accused of failing to carry out this last duty, which, according to his Republican detractors warranted the impeachment procedure against him in 1998. The question that triggered the impeachment proceedings was the president's finger wagging statement under oath that he "did not have sex with that woman."

In addition to these constitutionally sanctioned powers and duties, the president was also given two powers through an interpretation of the Constitution by the Supreme Court. Those two powers are those of issuing executive orders and of issuing executive agreements. The power of issuing executive orders was already discussed earlier. It was based on the case In re Neagle, of 1890. The power to issue executive agreements came about as a result of the case of United States v. Pink in 1942. Executive agreements are the equivalent of treaties but have no requirement of Senate approval attached to them. They are the international equivalent of executive orders.

In recognition of the expansion of the powers of the president, through an interpretation of the Constitution's implied powers, Congress has taken steps to limit the president's powers in several areas. As mentioned earlier, Congress most recently moved to rein in the presidential power of issuing executive orders it considers onerous. After the Watergate scandal, Congress moved to rein in the presidential power to wage war and to withhold funds for disbursement that Congress had already appropriated. President Nixon was considered guilty of having abused both these powers while in office. The one regarding expansion of the war in Vietnam into Cambodia and Laos, the other in order to put pressure on Congress to not fund programs he opposed. To counteract these presidential moves, Congress passed back to back the War Powers Resolution of 1973 and the Budget and Impoundment Control Act of 1974. While the intent of both was to curtail presidential wiggle room on matters that Congress had decided, the War Powers Act at least tacitly acknowledged that the president had the authority to commit U.S. troops abroad. The act simply mandated him to let Congress know of his intentions ahead of time, and then gave him time limits within which he had to terminate military action unless extended by Congress or unless Congress decided to declare war, in which case the president was free to commit troops until victory.

From the following list, and the ensuing discussion of each of these items, it becomes clear that the power of the president is limited but, in many instances, the president has a leading role in determining what the direction of government will be. Except for cases that are clearly delineated above, the president plays the role of leader in the sense of chief proposer of policy directions. Congress remains the most powerful branch, and in 1990s due to intense partisanship and dislike of the then occupant of the White House, became not just a persecutor of that president but a tool for the circumscription of the powers of the president in general. The move by Congress to curtail one of the few absolute powers of the president, the power to pardon, because of President Clinton's pardon of fugitive financier Mark Rich was only one example of Congress' assertion of its power over that of the presidency. In a similar sour mood after the fourth term in office of President Franklin Roosevelt, Congress under a Republican majority moved to curtail the term of the president to a maximum of two. Many Republicans in Congress have since regretted that amendment to the Constitution, since some of their most popular presidents or younger presidents such as George W. Bush could have benefited from a third term, as, of course, would some of the Democratic presidents, such as President Clinton.

A discussion of the presidency would not be complete without reference to the changes introduced during the now two terms of the presidency of President George W. Bush. When President Bush took office he spoke of a vision of his presidency and of the foreign policy of this country that would be "humbler" and more focused on the traditional values of Republicans at home. Things did indeed change with the attacks on New York and the Pentagon on September 11, 2001.

While it can be argued that conservatives had been planning to rebuild the power of the presidency ever since President Richard Nixon's departure from the White House in 1974, in order to recapture what under President Nixon was called the "Imperial Presidency" by historian Arthur Schlesinger Jr., certainly the development of the power of the presidency under President George W. Bush and Vice-President Cheney took even the most hardened observers of politics by surprise. Of course, nothing develops over night. The rebuilding of the power of the president was, as already stated, envisioned by the conservatives and their Republican allies already from the Ford presidency onward. It is instructive to look at the cast of characters that appeared in the Ford White House and to compare them to the cast of characters most associated with the spectacular expansion of the powers of the presidency under George W. Bush—Dick Cheney, President Ford's Chief of Staff, and Donald Rumsfeld, President Ford's Chief of Staff and Secretary of Defense, to name but two.

Among the developments leading to a notion of a strengthened and vigorous presidency one must mention the developments under President Reagan whose vision of the presidency as militarily assertive abroad and morally assertive at home, if necessary even in open conflict with Congress and in contravention of its will, resulted in the Iran-Contra scandal of 1987. A continuation of this vision was declared by President Bush senior on September 11, 1990, in a speech titled "The New World Order," where the president declared a new world order "where the rule of law not the law of the jungle governs the conduct of nations," and where a reinvigorated United Nations would bring about the vision of its founders of a peaceful world based on law with the United States as the leading power implementing this new world order. That new vision and the role of the United States in it was made possible by the disappearance of the Soviet Union, but also by the vision of a strengthened presidency that could lead the nation in this new global calling. The immediate aftermath of that new call was rather surprisingly the Gulf War against Saddam Hussein in 1991 and not a global international law inititiave.

A continuation of this vision was laid out in a document titled Project for the New American Century (PNAC) in 1997, which, since it focused again on America's foreign policy role in the world, put the role of the presidency center stage in shaping this global future. All these developments however paled in comparison to the perfect storm that September 11, 2001, and the events subsequent to it created for the presidency of the United States.

Naturally, in times of military crisis, the presidency becomes the locus of power in the American political system. Given a crisis, it is not prudent for 535 representatives to second-guess each other and the president. Action must be taken since the nation could be at risk. Given the predilections and preferences of conservatives and Republicans regarding the power of the presidency, the confluence of the attacks of September 11, 2001, and the control of the Congress and the White House by the Republican party, created a "perfect storm" regarding the rebuilding of the power of the presidency. In times of crisis the nation naturally rallies around its leader and the natural hesitancies of civil libertarians are suspended because of the need to respond to crisis. This confluence of events, together with the preferences expressed by the president and vice-president for a more vigorous presidency, resulted in the president and vice-president assuming what are now considered unprecedented powers. The necessity for this increase in powers for the office of the president has been explained and argued under the rubric of unitary executive, a term championed by among others, Justice Antonin Scalia, former attorney-general and presidential counselor Alberto Gonzales, Vice-President Dick Cheney, and President Bush himself.

The theory of unitary executive holds that the president is the sole holder of executive power according to the Constitution of the United States and further, that the president should not be challenged in his decisions by the Congress, especially in times of crisis where his leadership is required and vital to the security of the United States. This vision of a unitary executive has been expressed by presidents in a variety of ways. President Nixon used to speak of inherent powers of the presidency and stated once that "if the President does it, it is constitutional." Other presidents, Democrat and Republican alike, have used the power of the executive order to steer the policy of the government in their preferred direction and thus to contravene or short circuit Congress' prerogative of legislation. Other presidents have used the power of signing statements (President George W. Bush's preferred, though not exclusive, instrument of assertion of presidential prerogative). A signing statement is similar to the line-item veto or the practice used by President Nixon of impounding funds after Congress had appropriated them and designated them for expenditures. A signing statement is a statement by the president on a piece of legislation that he will carry it out with the following reservations, or not carry it out at all *even though* he is signing it into law thus effectively avoiding an override of this "virtual" veto and getting his way on the legislation as if it had been written just the way he wanted it to be written.

When a president has a friendly Congress to deal with, then the question of his power and his capacity to do as he pleases rarely if ever arises. President George W. Bush did not veto any legislation in the first five years of his term. He also faced no question on his conduct from Congress. He only vetoed one bill in his fifth year on the question of stem-cell research and has been vetoing some bills since the 2006 election (eight as of March 8, 2008) because Democrats have regained the upper hand in the House and the Senate. The last and most recent veto of the president dealt with a matter related to the expanded vision of presidential prerogative in that the president vetoed a bill on the executive's power to "forcefully interrogate" on March 8, 2008. Congress in this latest bill wished to declare the use of "waterboarding" (a technique of simulated drowning used on prisoners held by the CIA and other agencies of the executive branch under the aegis of the "War on Terror") illegal. Incidentally as a sign of the times, President Bush suffered three overrides of this vetoes since November 2007. The latest override in July 2008 was on his veto on the medicure Bill most members of congress favored.

The expanded powers of the presidency under President George W. Bush have been directly related to the so-called War on Terror resulting from the attacks of September 11, 2001. They have included claims of exemptions by the vice-president and the president from scrutiny by Congress into their decisions, with the vice-president even going so far as to claim at one point that he is not a member of the executive branch at all but rather of the legislative branch given that his pay check comes from the Senate and that he has the constitutional responsibility of casting tie-breaking votes, thus making him a member of the legislative with the attendant legislative immunity that goes with the office. They have further included creations of new categories of legal status for prisoners in the War on Terror, called "unlawful enemy combatants," which effectively put these prisoners in a legal limbo allowing them to be "forcefully interrogated" and held *incommunicado* without recourse (see *habeas corpus* discussions above) at off-shore locations such as Guantanamo, Cuba. They have also included claims of necessity of wiretapping of citizens without congressional or court oversight, even of the most minimal kind as required under the Foreign Intelligence Surveillance Act (FISA) of 1978, and have created major challenges to dearly held notions of civil liberties, let alone to notions of congressional prerogative, that have been at the foundation of government of the United States since its beginning.

Given these developments, the question will be how long will the trend of expansion of presidential power and prerogative continue. Given the open ended nature of the War on Terror and unwillingness or inability of Congress to assert its will unequivocally on the question of separation of powers and checks and balances, the pendulum swing toward more presidential power may not yet have reached its highest point.

Next let us look at the least dangerous of the three branches, the judicial branch.

CHAPTER 14

The Judicial Branch

A study of the judicial branch of government must inevitably focus on the relationship of power between this branch and the other two branches already discussed. As mentioned in the lecture on Congress, the Founding Fathers explicitly made Congress the first branch of government and endowed it with exceptional powers in its own right. Not only that, they also endowed it with power over the other two branches. That fact is discussed both in these lectures and in the textbooks under the rubric "checks and balances." There is one essential element to checks and balances, however, that the Founding Fathers did not include in the letter and text of the constitution at all, namely, the capacity of this third branch, the judiciary, to check the other two. In fact most everything about this third branch is peculiar and different from the other two. Let us have a brief look at the judiciary with these points in mind.

The first thing we realize about the judicial branch is that it is the only one of the three branches of government that is not elected by the people. This is not an unusual fact, as many of the judiciaries around the world are not elected but, on the other hand, in the states of the Union, there are many judiciaries that are, such as the Supreme Court of California. The next thing we realize is that the federal judiciary does not play the same role as the other two branches in the policy-making process. It comes into play only when there is a crisis or question about the process, the other two, on the other hand, are involved in the process routinely and essentially.

In terms of composition and in terms of requirements for office, the judiciary also differs from the other two branches. The members of the Supreme Court are appointed by the president and confirmed by the Senate, but the qualifications for judges to be able to be considered for the position are not stated in the Constitution. Unlike the other two branches, the only thing the Constitution states about the occupants of the seats on the Supreme Court is: "The judges, both of the supreme and inferior Courts, shall hold their Offices during good Behavior, and shall, at stated Times, receive for their services, a Compensation, which shall not be diminished during their Continuance in Office" (Article III, section 1). The notion of "good behavior" refers to the fact that they hold their office for life, except if impeached, and this in itself is noteworthy. Not only are they not elected but they can also not be removed, except for breaking the law, which, of course goes without saying! The question of qualifications for office for judges is not raised in the constitution, presumably, because the other two branches have so much say over who becomes a judge, that the Founding Fathers felt it redundant to detail what those are. An individual who would lack the requisite experience and the legal qualifications to be a Justice on the Supreme Court would not pass through the two obstacles of a presidential nomination and a scrutiny by the Senate, still in politically contentious times, less than qualified individuals could get by this process simply based on their party loyalty.

Qualifications of justices aside, as mentioned earlier, the Court has not been equipped by the Founding Fathers with the power to review the acts of the other two branches in the same way that they have expressly been in the letter of the constitution. This is an odd fact, and it led to great despair with the entire court on the part of the first Supreme Court Chief Justice, John Jay, who in 1795 resigned in disgust over the fact that the Court had no power whatsoever to carry out its mandate as he saw it. Indeed, the Court has no power of checking the other two branches. Here is what the Constitution says the Court has power to do. According to the Constitution, the Court has jurisdiction over all matters "arising under this Constitution, the laws of the United States, and Treaties made, or which shall be made, under their Authority."

Particularly, the Court has two kinds of "jurisdiction," or power, to speak: one called "original," meaning that cases begin and end in the Supreme Court, and those cases are cases involving diplomats and when a "State shall be Party"; the other, "appellate," meaning the Court becomes the court of last resort after all the other levels have been appealed to and exhausted, both on the federal side, if the case be federal, and on the state side, if the case be a state case. Nothing in the foregoing points, however, states that the Court has any formal power over the other two branches such as confirming any of the occupants therein, or that the Court has the power to second-guess the other two branches when it comes to their acts and the constitutionality of those acts. The fact that the other two branches can act unconstitutionally, however, is a distinct possibility, and it seems that the Founding Fathers did not consider that possibility seriously enough, or, as defenders of congressional power would hold, that the Founding Fathers felt that Congress' word would be the overriding word and, thus, in a sense, constitutional *ipso facto*. While that sentiment is understandable, it is not correct, as the American system differs in this specifically from the British one in that here a written constitution is the arbiter of the political game and, unlike the British parliament, acts of Congress are not *ipso facto* constitutional.

It was, as a matter of fact, an act of Congress passed in February 1801, concerning the District of Columbia and the appointment of justices of the peace in that district, that first raised the possibility of such a conflict. It was also this act and the resulting complaint dealing with its mandate, that created the power of the Court to declare acts of Congress, at first, and then later acts of the president unconstitutional. The case was *Marbury v. Madison* (1803) and the person who created this power for the Court was Chief Justice John Marshall.

The case revolved around two questions: Did Marbury have a right to his commission given to him by President Adams and denied him by President Jefferson; and second, did the court have jurisdiction in this case at all? Marshall answered the first question in the affirmative, but answered the second in the negative, stating that the law pursuant to which Marbury came to seek remedy before the Court, mandated the Court to do something that it could not do under the Constitution, namely, to hear a case on original jurisdiction when this was not such a case. But then Marshall went on, and took the opportunity to say the words that would give the Court power that it did not possess under the letter of the Constitution but that he felt it needed to have, and indeed did already have in the spirit of the Constitution. Marshall stated:

> *It is emphatically the province and duty of the judicial department to say what the law is. Those who apply the rule to particular cases, must of necessity expound and interpret that rule. If two laws conflict with each other the courts must decide on the operation of each.*

> *So if a law be in opposition to the constitution; if both the law and the constitution apply to a particular case, so that the court must either decide that case conformably to the law, disregarding the constitution; or conformably to the constitution, disregarding the law; the court must determine which of these conflicting rules governs the case. This is of the very essence of judicial duty.*

> *Thus, the particular phraseology of the constitution of the United States confirms and strengthens the principle, supposed to be essential to all written constitutions, that a law repugnant to the constitution is void; and that courts, as well as other departments, are bound by that instrument."* (Marbury v. Madison, 1803)

With these words, the power of judicial review was created for the Court, which helped complete the cycle of checks and balances by extending to the third branch as well.

Courts are often considered the guarantors of freedom and justice in a political system. Courts are also considered the least dangerous of the three branches, as traditionally courts have been the institutions to uphold the rights of the people and the executives have been the ones to use their sword to harm them. In the case of the U.S. Supreme Court, not only did the court assume its traditional role of upholder of the law but it also became the guarantor of the Constitution and the arbiter over what the Constitution was and was not.

CHAPTER 15

Civil Rights and Civil Liberties

The discussion of civil rights and civil liberties is often tied in with that of federalism, and rightly so. Civil liberties and civil rights debates are intricately linked to the federalism debate because the structure of the territorial arrangement in the United States brings up the potential question of overlaps of sovereignty, as well as that of separate spheres of sovereignty. The granting of civil rights and civil liberties, as an act by one of these levels of government, may or may not translate to the other necessarily. The questions of what rights apply where and which level of government is the appropriate grantor of which rights have always been intriguing ones in the American context.

During the early phase of federalism, into the 1920s, and even beyond with regard to civil rights into the early 1950s, the question of civil liberties and civil rights was regarded as one to be resolved appropriately at the state level. In other words, states were left free to decide what privileges and immunities they would grant their citizens and which ones they would not. This despite a civil war that was supposed to have resolved, in part at least, the question in favor of the national government. From the New Deal era onward and onto the 1970s, the national government's list of civil liberties and civil rights became the frame of reference for the states as well. From 1974 to today, that trend has slowly been reversing with the ascent of "new federalism." States-rights advocates have gained more and more power and, in conjunction with that, a state's freedom to pick and choose which of the federal civil liberties and civil rights it would enforce and which it would not has increased. In the last three years of the twentieth century, the Supreme Court consistently rolled back federal power in civil rights cases, culminating most recently in a ruling against an employee of the University of Alabama seeking redress under the Americans with Disabilities Act (USSC *Univ. of Alabama v. Garrett* [2/21/2001]). We have come, it seems, full circle in the civil rights and civil liberties debate.

Before we elaborate on these points any further, let us go back to the beginning and define civil rights and civil liberties. We will then take a closer look at the debate around the nationalization of the Bill of Rights and then will devote some time to the development of civil rights from the Fourteenth Amendment onward, through *Plessy v. Ferguson, Brown v. Board of Education of Topeka, Kansas,* and beyond. We will end that examination with some remarks on the future of civil rights and civil liberties in the United States.

Civil liberties can be defined as a set of freedoms granted the people by the government in the form of injunctions against excessive government interference and abuse. Civil liberties are those things citizens are free to do in a society, but they are also those things government is not free to legislate against, within reasonable boundaries, of course.

Why are civil liberties called "civil liberties" if they are enshrined in a document called the Bill of *Rights*? They are called civil liberties because they refer to a people's *freedoms* or *liberties*. Those liberties, however, are also referred to as a people's *rights* as against the government. Thus the notion of a Bill of Rights of the people. So why not call them civil rights to begin with? Indeed, that is a good question. They have not been called that because the notion of liberties was strong in the revolutionary language, and only secondarily the notion of rights. It was not "give me rights or give me death" that fanned the flames of revolution and set the imagination on fire, it was "give me liberty or give me death!" Liberty is one of the two great principles of democracy, and thus civil liberties are a reflection and celebration of this fact. On the other hand, why was that list in which the liberties were listed not called the Bill of Liberties then? Perhaps because the phrase Bill of Liberties did not sound as right as that of Bill of Rights, but certainly because legally speaking, these principles enshrined in the Constitution of the United States are, in fact, legal rights that can be claimed from the government of the United States, whereas liberties are more abstract and perhaps more philosophical principles, and do not carry the same legal connotation with them as "rights" do.

What, on the other hand, are civil rights? Civil rights are rights and privileges that citizens have successfully claimed from government subsequent to the establishment of that government, and which government has been willing to grant them. These rights, unlike civil liberties, are not claimed by individuals but by groups, of which individual members will then be beneficiaries. These rights are not only rights that individuals claim from government, they are also protections that individuals ask for, from government, as against other groups or individuals who might discriminate against them. The notion of civil rights is a manifestation of the dictum by Thomas Jefferson that democracy is not just majority rule but also minority rights; that without minority rights, democracy would turn into "tyranny of the majority," a form of government that is just as bad as its namesake, tyranny by one! Civil rights and the rights of minorities within a democracy are inseparable notions.

The story of civil rights is the story of the development and maturation of a democracy. Civil rights, in a sense, can be considered an extension of the original list of rights enshrined in the founding documents of democracies. In America, however, the two are separate and referred to by different names as America was the first country to experiment with the granting of civil liberties as part of its constitution and the expansion of those rights through its various civil rights movements. Other countries, benefiting from the American experience, were often able to put a longer list of rights of the people in their documents, and do often include the notion of equality and the protection against discrimination into their constitutions. When pioneering something, one does not have the benefit of learning from others in order to get it right the first time around. On the other hand, the glory of it is that much greater.

In the past several years, New Zealand, Australia, Canada, and the United Kingdom have looked at the American example in search for a Bill of Rights for their own citizens. The European Union, on the other hand, incorporated both the notion of civil liberties and civil rights in its recent European Charter of Human Rights, that has now become European law, above and beyond the national laws of the member states of the Union.

When discussing civil liberties, textbooks usually focus on the Bill of Rights and a detailed discussion of how each of the first ten amendments to the Constitution can and have been interpreted by the Supreme Court over the years. One of the first things students find out is that there are no absolute rights in the political arena. Civil liberties are positive rights and thus relative. They are positive because they have been promulgated by government. They are relative because they have been interpreted and curtailed as government has seen fit. There is a threshold, of course, below which government cannot go and still claim to be a free government, but that threshold has been quite flexible very often.

The more interesting matter has been the counterintuitive notion, in the United States, that rights enshrined in the Bill of Rights may not be available to all citizens everywhere, when they are not dealing with the United States government but rather with their state governments. This notion is counterintuitive because we do not tend to think of ourselves as citizens of two separate sovereign entities coexisting side by side, and yet that is the interpretation that seems to be resurfacing in the new Supreme Court decisions coming out of the court in recent days. The first individual to test this hypothesis and to find out to his dismay that indeed there were two separate and distinct spheres of sovereignty, was Barron, who in his suit against the city of Baltimore and the state of Maryland in 1833, maintained that the U.S. Constitution's Fifth Amendment protection against seizure of property without just compensation applied to his case. The city had dumped sand in the waterway, diverting the course of the water and making his docks unusable. He sued the city and his case came before the Supreme Court. In his opinion in that matter, Chief Justice John Marshall argued that the Fifth Amendment protection was a protection against actions by the national government and not against those of the states, and that unless the states had anything in their state constitutions to that effect also, the national constitution would not apply in cases like that of Barron. The doctrine that the court maintained in that decision, was the doctrine of dual sovereignty and its corollary, dual citizenship, which meant that states were free not to follow the U.S. Constitution if they chose to. This, of course, coincided with the doctrine of dual federalism, which stated much the same with regard to the relationship between the national government and the states, and the Court's decision in *Barron* was thus only a reflection of the political reality of the time, as Marshall's arguments in the case clearly show. (see Appendix G for text of *Barron v. Baltimore* [1833].)

To remedy the situation of dual citizenship and the commensurate right of the states to interpret the laws on a different standard than those of the national government, the Fourteenth Amendment was added to the constitution right after the Civil War. In a sense, the Civil War was fought over this very matter, whether there were two nations side by side, or even just two nations separately, or whether there was only one, in which there were entities called states under one union. The question, as every student of American history knows, was not settled in the halls of academia or in the court rooms, it was settled on the battlefield and the union side won. And as all such victories go, the other side remained unconvinced despite the fact that it did not have anymore choice in the matter.

The Fourteenth Amendment, however, is a strange remedy, given that it could have been written much more unambiguously under the circumstances of the victory of the North. In order to remedy the ills of dual citizenship, it states: "All persons born or naturalized in the United States, and subject to the jurisdiction thereof, are citizens of the United States," but then continues "and of the states wherein they reside," thus recreating the very ambiguity it meant to dispel with the first half of the sentence. It does continue to state, however: "No state shall make or enforce any law which shall abridge the privileges or immunities of citizens of the United States," and even goes on to address some of poor Barron's concerns regarding the taking of property without due process, but too late, of course, for his dilemma. It culminates in the phrase for which it is most known perhaps, that no state may deny "any person within its jurisdiction the equal protection of the laws." This clause is the only place in the Constitution where the word "equality" is used. It is also the bedrock from which the civil rights movement has drawn its strength.

What the Fourteenth Amendment did among other things, was to make possible that the Bill of Rights be brought to the states and made applicable to them. This notion was called the "Nationalization of the Bill of Rights." Armed with the wording of this amendment, cases were brought before the Supreme Court starting in 1897 on the very question Barron sued for, "eminent domain" and its corollary "just compensation," and they have continued to our day, though not always in the same direction as hoped for by Barron. By 1973, with the case of *Roe v. Wade,* all important civil liberties in the Bill of Rights had been nationalized, including one, the right to privacy, that was not even in the Bill of Rights. It was not in the actual wording of the Bill of Rights, but there in its spirit, as the Supreme Court justices held in that case. Besides the Fourteenth Amendment, the Court also used the commerce clause of Article 1, section 8, to impose on the states many of the provisions of the Bill of Rights that states considered burdensome on them. The commerce clause was also often used to nationalize civil rights such as the Americans with Disabilities Act of 1990, but as we have also seen, with the conservative majority in the U.S. Supreme Court and with the conservative majorities in the Congress, the Court has also been willing to reverse this trend quite dramatically in the last few years.

Reversal of the trend toward a national standard, however, is not just a recent phenomenon. The history of the fight for civil rights in America is illustrative of this point here. The most spectacular reversal in the trend toward national standards occurred in 1896, when in the case of *Plessy v. Ferguson*, the U.S. Supreme Court held that the equal protection clause of the Fourteenth Amendment did not apply to individuals, and then in an amazing further twist held that races have a right and ought to be separate from each other, creating thus the doctrine of "separate but equal" in contradiction to everything the nation had just gone through barely a generation before. The *Plessy* decision was indeed a low point in the trend towards a reversal of the gains made through victory in the Civil War, but it was a natural development from the strong resentment that had still been festering in the South among whites that hated the post–Civil War reality. *Plessy's* political reality would tear the nation apart for many many years to come, well into the second half of the twentieth century (see Appendix for *Plessy v. Ferguson* [1896] and also Judge Harlan's lone dissent in that case).

Plessy had meant legalization of segregation and segregation meant treating blacks as second class citizens. It took almost sixty years of misery for blacks to be able to successfully challenge segregation, and it was a young lawyer by the name of Thurgood Marshall, who was to be the hero for the cause of equality and integration. Thurgood Marshall who had been hired by the NAACP to fight for the abolition of segregation saw his chance in a case from Topeka, Kansas, where schools, as most everywhere else in the nation, were segregated but kept scrupulously equal in access and availability of facilities. Thurgood Marshall's argument before the Warren Court was that segregation itself created a condition of inequality on the minority race, and that equalizing facilities was no remedy to that reality. Chief Justice Earl Warren reiterated that logic in his opinion in *Brown v. Board of Education of Topeka, Kansas* (see Appendix J for full text), when he stated:

> We come then to the question presented: Does segregation of children in public schools solely on the basis of race, even though the physical facilities and other "tangible" factors may be equal, deprive the children of the minority group of equal educational opportunities? We believe that it does. . . .
>
> Segregation of white and colored children in public schools has a detrimental effect upon the colored children. The impact is greater when it has the sanction of the law, for the policy of separating the races is usually interpreted as denoting the inferiority of the negro group. A sense of inferiority affects the motivation of a child to learn. Segregation with the sanction of law, therefore, has a tendency to [retard] the educational and mental development of negro children and to deprive them of some of the benefits they would receive in a racially integrated school system. (Brown v. Board of Education, 1954)

With *Brown v. Board of Education,* the civil rights movement gained the legal momentum it needed for a further assault on the vestiges of inequality in

America. The civil rights movement itself gave rise to an ever expanding circle of what Lowi and Ginsberg have called the "rise of the politics of rights," including more and more groups under the umbrella of civil rights. As with every trend, this rise also created a countermovement for the curtailment of the faster and faster extension of rights to newer and newer groups. One of the landmark cases reversing the advance of rights of minorities in the late 1970s, was of course the case of Bakke against the University of California, Davis, in 1978. That case introduced the notion of "reverse discrimination," and heralded the reversal trend that we have seen playing itself out before our eyes in the last twenty years, culminating in the abolition of affirmative action standards in California in 1997. The question before us today will be: Will there be a conservative latter-day Earl Warren waiting in the wings to be appointed by a latter-day Dwight Eisenhower, who will turn out to be the kind of friend of civil rights as Earl Warren became, or will we continue on the present trend towards more and more states rights on the question of civil rights and more and more federal government power to restrict civil liberties? Only time will tell.

Appendix A

THE MODIFIED ALMOND AND POWELL MODEL OF THE POLITICAL SYSTEM

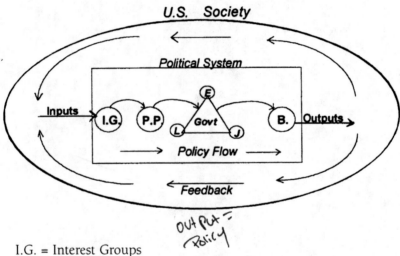

I.G. = Interest Groups
P.P. = Political Parties
Govt = Government
E = Executive Branch
L = Legislative Branch
J = Judicial Branch
B = Bureaucracy

Note: I am very grateful to my Teaching Assistant Katerina Zamyatina for the design of the model, which she has used in her instruction of students in the American Government classes.

 # Appendix B

THE DECLARATION OF INDEPENDENCE (EXCERPTS)
Thomas Jefferson (1776)

When in the Course of human events, it becomes necessary for one people to dissolve the political bands which have connected them with another, and to assume among the powers of the earth, the separate and equal station to which the Laws of Nature and of Nature's God entitle them, a decent respect to the opinions of mankind requires that they should declare the causes which impel them to the separation.

We hold these truths to be self-evident, that all men are created equal, that they are endowed by their Creator with certain unalienable Rights, that among these are Life, Liberty and the pursuit of Happiness.—That to secure these rights, Governments are instituted among Men, deriving their just powers from the consent of the governed,—That whenever any Form of Government becomes destructive of these ends, it is the Right of the People to alter or to abolish it, and to institute new Government, laying its foundation on such principles and organizing its powers in such form, as to them shall seem most likely to effect their Safety and Happiness. Prudence, indeed, will dictate that Governments long established should not be changed for light and transient causes; and accordingly all experience hath shewn, that mankind are more disposed to suffer, while evils are sufferable, than to right themselves by abolishing the forms to which they are accustomed. But when a long train of abuses and usurpations, pursuing invariably the same Object evinces a design to reduce them under absolute Despotism, it is their right, it is their duty, to throw off such Government, and to provide new Guards for their future security.—Such has been the patient sufferance of these Colonies; and such is now the necessity which constrains them to alter their former Systems of Government. The history of the present King of Great Britain is a history of repeated injuries and usurpations, all having in direct object the establishment of an absolute Tyranny over these States.

 # Appendix C

FEDERALIST NO. 10
James Madison

The Union as a Safeguard Against Domestic Faction and Insurrection
Friday, November 23, 1787.

To the People of the State of New York:

AMONG the numerous advantages promised by a well constructed Union, none deserves to be more accurately developed than its tendency to break and control the violence of faction. The friend of popular governments never finds himself so much alarmed for their character and fate, as when he contemplates their propensity to this dangerous vice. He will not fail, therefore, to set a due value on any plan which, without violating the principles to which he is attached, provides a proper cure for it. The instability, injustice, and confusion introduced into the public councils, have, in truth, been the mortal diseases under which popular governments have everywhere perished; as they continue to be the favorite and fruitful topics from which the adversaries to liberty derive their most specious declamations. The valuable improvements made by the American constitutions on the popular models, both ancient and modern, cannot certainly be too much admired; but it would be an unwarrantable partiality, to contend that they have as effectually obviated the danger on this side, as was wished and expected. Complaints are everywhere heard from our most considerate and virtuous citizens, equally the friends of public and private faith, and of public and personal liberty, that our governments are too unstable, that the public good is disregarded in the conflicts of rival parties, and that measures are too often decided, not according to the rules of justice and the rights of the minor party, but by the superior force of an interested and overbearing majority. However anxiously we may wish that these complaints had no foundation, the evidence, of known facts will not permit us to deny that they are in some degree true. It will be found, indeed, on a candid review of our situation, that some of the distresses under which we labor have been erroneously charged on the operation of our governments; but it will be found, at the same time, that other causes will not alone account for many of our heaviest misfortunes; and, particularly, for that prevailing and increasing distrust of public engagements, and alarm for private rights, which are echoed from one end of the continent to the other. These must be chiefly, if not wholly, effects of the unsteadiness and injustice with which a factious spirit has tainted our public administrations.

By a faction, I understand a number of citizens, whether amounting to a majority or a minority of the whole, who are united and actuated by some common impulse of passion, or of interest, adversed to the rights of other citizens, or to the permanent and aggregate interests of the community.

There are two methods of curing the mischiefs of faction: the one, by removing its causes; the other, by controlling its effects.

There are again two methods of removing the causes of faction: the one, by destroying the liberty which is essential to its existence; the other, by giving to every citizen the same opinions, the same passions, and the same interests.

It could never be more truly said than of the first remedy, that it was worse than the disease. Liberty is to faction what air is to fire, an aliment without which it instantly expires. But it could not be less folly to abolish liberty, which is essential to political life, because it nourishes faction, than it would be to wish the annihilation of air, which is essential to animal life, because it imparts to fire its destructive agency.

The second expedient is as impracticable as the first would be unwise. As long as the reason of man continues fallible, and he is at liberty to exercise it, different opinions will be formed. As long as the connection subsists between his reason and his self-love, his opinions and his passions will have a reciprocal influence on each other; and the former will be objects to which the latter will attach themselves. The diversity in the faculties of men, from which the rights of property originate, is not less an insuperable obstacle to a uniformity of interests. The protection of these faculties is the first object of government. From the protection of different and unequal faculties of acquiring property, the possession of different degrees and kinds of property immediately results; and from the influence of these on the sentiments and views of the respective proprietors, ensues a division of the society into different interests and parties.

The latent causes of faction are thus sown in the nature of man; and we see them everywhere brought into different degrees of activity, according to the different circumstances of civil society. A zeal for different opinions concerning religion, concerning government, and many other points, as well of speculation as of practice; an attachment to different leaders ambitiously contending for pre-eminence and power; or to persons of other descriptions whose fortunes have been interesting to the human passions, have, in turn, divided mankind into parties, inflamed them with mutual animosity, and rendered them much more disposed to vex and oppress each other than to co-operate for their common good. So strong is this propensity of mankind to fall into mutual animosities, that where no substantial occasion presents itself, the most frivolous and fanciful distinctions have been sufficient to kindle their unfriendly passions and excite their most violent conflicts. But the most common and durable source of factions has been the various and unequal distribution of property. Those who hold and those who are without property have ever formed distinct interests in society. Those who are creditors, and those who are debtors, fall under a like discrimination. A landed interest, a manufacturing interest, a mercantile interest, a moneyed interest, with many lesser interests, grow up of necessity in civilized nations, and divide them into different classes, actuated by different sentiments and views. The regulation of these various and interfering interests forms the principal task of modern legislation, and involves the spirit of party and faction in the necessary and ordinary operations of the government.

No man is allowed to be a judge in his own cause, because his interest would certainly bias his judgment, and, not improbably, corrupt his integrity. With equal, nay with greater reason, a body of men are unfit to be both judges and parties at the same time; yet what are many of the most important acts of legislation, but so many judicial determinations, not indeed concerning the rights of single persons, but concerning the rights of large bodies of citizens? And what are the different classes of legislators but advocates and parties to the causes which they determine? Is a law proposed concerning private debts? It is a question to which the creditors are parties on one side and the debtors on the other. Justice ought to hold the balance between them. Yet the parties are, and must be, themselves the judges; and the most numerous party, or, in other words, the most powerful faction must be expected to prevail. Shall domestic manufactures be encouraged, and in what degree, by restrictions on foreign manufactures? are questions which would be differently decided by the landed and the manufacturing classes, and probably by neither with a sole regard to justice and the public good. The apportionment of taxes on the various descriptions of property is an act which seems to require the most exact impartiality; yet there is, perhaps, no legislative act in which greater opportunity and temptation are given to a predominant party to trample on the rules of justice. Every shilling with which they overburden the inferior number, is a shilling saved to their own pockets.

It is in vain to say that enlightened statesmen will be able to adjust these clashing interests, and render them all subservient to the public good. Enlightened statesmen will not always be at the helm. Nor, in many cases, can such an adjustment be made at all without taking into view indirect and remote considerations, which will rarely prevail over the immediate interest which one party may find in disregarding the rights of another or the good of the whole.

The inference to which we are brought is, that the causes of faction cannot be removed, and that relief is only to be sought in the means of controlling its effects.

If a faction consists of less than a majority, relief is supplied by the republican principle, which enables the majority to defeat its sinister views by regular vote. It may clog the administration, it may convulse the society; but it will be unable to execute and mask its violence under the forms of the Constitution. When a majority is included in a faction, the form of popular government, on the other hand, enables it to sacrifice to its ruling passion or interest both the public good and the rights of other citizens. To secure the public good and private rights against the danger of such a faction, and at the same time to preserve the spirit and the form of popular government, is then the great object to which our inquiries are directed. Let me add that it is the great desideratum by which this form of government can be rescued from the opprobrium under which it has so long labored, and be recommended to the esteem and adoption of mankind.

By what means is this object attainable? Evidently by one of two only. Either the existence of the same passion or interest in a majority at the same time must be prevented, or the majority, having such coexistent passion or interest, must be rendered, by their number and local situation, unable to concert and carry into effect schemes of oppression. If the impulse and the opportunity be suffered to coincide, we well know that neither moral nor religious motives can be relied on as an adequate control. They are not found to be such on the injustice and violence of individuals, and lose their efficacy in proportion to the number combined together, that is, in proportion as their efficacy becomes needful.

From this view of the subject it may be concluded that a pure democracy, by which I mean a society consisting of a small number of citizens, who assemble and administer the government in person, can admit of no cure for the mischiefs of faction. A common passion or interest will, in almost every case, be felt by a majority of the whole; a communication and concert result from the form of government itself; and there is nothing to check the inducements to sacrifice the weaker party or an obnoxious individual. Hence it is that such democracies have ever been spectacles of turbulence and contention; have ever been found incompatible with personal security or the rights of property; and have in general been as short in their lives as they have been violent in their deaths. Theoretic politicians, who have patronized this species of government, have erroneously supposed that by reducing mankind to a perfect equality in their political rights, they would, at the same time, be perfectly equalized and assimilated in their possessions, their opinions, and their passions.

A republic, by which I mean a government in which the scheme of representation takes place, opens a different prospect, and promises the cure for which we are seeking. Let us examine the points in which it varies from pure democracy, and we shall comprehend both the nature of the cure and the efficacy which it must derive from the Union.

The two great points of difference between a democracy and a republic are: first, the delegation of the government, in the latter, to a small number of citizens elected by the rest; secondly, the greater number of citizens, and greater sphere of country, over which the latter may be extended.

The effect of the first difference is, on the one hand, to refine and enlarge the public views, by passing them through the medium of a chosen body of citizens, whose wisdom may best discern the true interest of their country, and whose patriotism and love of justice will be least likely to sacrifice it to temporary or partial considerations. Under such a regulation, it may well happen that the public voice, pronounced by the representatives of the people, will be more consonant to the public good than if pronounced by the people themselves, convened for the purpose. On the other hand, the effect may be inverted. Men of factious tempers, of local prejudices, or of sinister designs, may, by intrigue, by corruption, or by other means, first obtain the suffrages, and then betray the interests, of the people. The question resulting is, whether small or extensive republics are more favorable to the election of proper guardians of the public weal; and it is clearly decided in favor of the latter by two obvious considerations:

In the first place, it is to be remarked that, however small the republic may be, the representatives must be raised to a certain number, in order to guard against the cabals of a few; and that, however large it may be, they must be limited to a certain number, in order to guard against the confusion of a multitude. Hence, the number of representatives in the two cases not being in proportion to that of the two constituents, and being proportionally greater in the small republic, it follows that, if the proportion of fit characters be not less in the large than in the small republic, the former will present a greater option, and consequently a greater probability of a fit choice.

In the next place, as each representative will be chosen by a greater number of citizens in the large than in the small republic, it will be more difficult for unworthy candidates to practice with success the vicious arts by which elections are too often carried; and the suffrages of the people being more free, will be more likely to centre in men who possess the most attractive merit and the most diffusive and established characters.

It must be confessed that in this, as in most other cases, there is a mean, on both sides of which inconveniences will be found to lie. By enlarging too much the number of electors, you render the representatives too little acquainted with all their local circumstances and lesser interests; as by reducing it too much, you render him unduly attached to these, and too little fit to comprehend and pursue great and national objects. The federal Constitution forms a happy combination in this respect; the great and aggregate interests being referred to the national, the local and particular to the State legislatures.

The other point of difference is, the greater number of citizens and extent of territory which may be brought within the compass of republican than of democratic government; and it is this circumstance principally which renders factious combinations less to be dreaded in the former than in the latter. The smaller the society, the fewer probably will be the distinct parties and interests composing it; the fewer the distinct parties and interests, the more frequently will a majority be found of the same party; and the smaller the number of individuals composing a majority, and the smaller the compass within which they are placed, the more easily will they concert and execute their plans of oppression. Extend the sphere, and you take in a greater variety of parties and interests; you make it less probable that a majority of the whole will have a common motive to invade the rights of other citizens; or if such a common motive exists, it will be more difficult for all who feel it to discover their own strength, and to act in unison with each other. Besides other impediments, it may be remarked that, where there is a consciousness of unjust or dishonorable purposes, communication is always checked by distrust in proportion to the number whose concurrence is necessary.

Hence, it clearly appears, that the same advantage which a republic has over a democracy, in controlling the effects of faction, is enjoyed by a large over a small republic,—is enjoyed by the Union over the States composing it. Does the advantage consist in the substitution of representatives whose enlightened views and virtuous sentiments render them superior to local prejudices and schemes of injustice? It will not be denied that the representation of the Union will be most likely to possess these requisite endowments. Does it consist in the greater security afforded by a greater variety of parties, against the event of any one party being able to outnumber and oppress the rest? In an equal degree does the increased variety of parties comprised within the Union, increase this security. Does it, in fine, consist in the greater obstacles opposed to the concert and accomplishment of the secret wishes of an unjust and interested majority? Here, again, the extent of the Union gives it the most palpable advantage.

The influence of factious leaders may kindle a flame within their particular States, but will be unable to spread a general conflagration through the other States. A religious sect may degenerate into a political faction in a part of the Confederacy; but the variety of sects dispersed over the entire face of it must secure the national councils against any danger from that source. A rage for paper money, for an abolition of debts, for an equal division of property, or for any other improper or wicked project, will be less apt to pervade the whole body of the Union than a particular member of it; in the same proportion as such a malady is more likely to taint a particular county or district, than an entire State.

In the extent and proper structure of the Union, therefore, we behold a republican remedy for the diseases most incident to republican government. And according to the degree of pleasure and pride we feel in being republicans, ought to be our zeal in cherishing the spirit and supporting the character of federalists.

Publius

 # Appendix D

FEDERALIST NO. 51
James Madison (or Alexander Hamilton)

The Structure of the Government Must Furnish the Proper Checks and Balances Between the Different Departments
Friday, February 8, 1788.

To the People of the State of New York:

To what expedient, then, shall we finally resort, for maintaining in practice the necessary partition of power among the several departments, as laid down in the Constitution? The only answer that can be given is, that as all these exterior provisions are found to be inadequate, the defect must be supplied, by so contriving the interior structure of the government as that its several constituent parts may, by their mutual relations, be the means of keeping each other in their proper places. Without presuming to undertake a full development of this important idea, I will hazard a few general observations, which may perhaps place it in a clearer light, and enable us to form a more correct judgment of the principles and structure of the government planned by the convention.

In order to lay a due foundation for that separate and distinct exercise of the different powers of government, which to a certain extent is admitted on all hands to be essential to the preservation of liberty, it is evident that each department should have a will of its own; and consequently should be so constituted that the members of each should have as little agency as possible in the appointment of the members of the others. Were this principle rigorously adhered to, it would require that all the appointments for the supreme executive, legislative, and judiciary magistracies should be drawn from the same fountain of authority, the people, through channels having no communication whatever with one another. Perhaps such a plan of constructing the several departments would be less difficult in practice than it may in contemplation appear. Some difficulties, however, and some additional expense would attend the execution of it. Some deviations, therefore, from the principle must be admitted. In the constitution

101

of the judiciary department in particular, it might be inexpedient to insist rigorously on the principle: first, because peculiar qualifications being essential in the members, the primary consideration ought to be to select that mode of choice which best secures these qualifications; secondly, because the permanent tenure by which the appointments are held in that department, must soon destroy all sense of dependence on the authority conferring them.

It is equally evident, that the members of each department should be as little dependent as possible on those of the others, for the emoluments annexed to their offices. Were the executive magistrate, or the judges, not independent of the legislature in this particular, their independence in every other would be merely nominal.

But the great security against a gradual concentration of the several powers in the same department, consists in giving to those who administer each department the necessary constitutional means and personal motives to resist encroachments of the others. The provision for defense must in this, as in all other cases, be made commensurate to the danger of attack. Ambition must be made to counteract ambition. The interest of the man must be connected with the constitutional rights of the place. It may be a reflection on human nature, that such devices should be necessary to control the abuses of government. But what is government itself, but the greatest of all reflections on human nature? If men were angels, no government would be necessary. If angels were to govern men, neither external nor internal controls on government would be necessary. In framing a government which is to be administered by men over men, the great difficulty lies in this: you must first enable the government to control the governed; and in the next place oblige it to control itself. A dependence on the people is, no doubt, the primary control on the government; but experience has taught mankind the necessity of auxiliary precautions.

This policy of supplying, by opposite and rival interests, the defect of better motives, might be traced through the whole system of human affairs, private as well as public. We see it particularly displayed in all the subordinate distributions of power, where the constant aim is to divide and arrange the several offices in such a manner as that each may be a check on the other that the private interest of every individual may be a sentinel over the public rights. These inventions of prudence cannot be less requisite in the distribution of the supreme powers of the State.

But it is not possible to give to each department an equal power of self-defense. In republican government, the legislative authority necessarily predominates. The remedy for this inconveniency is to divide the legislature into different branches; and to render them, by different modes of election and different principles of action, as little connected with each other as the nature of their common functions and their common dependence on the society will admit. It may even be necessary to guard against dangerous encroachments by still further precautions. As the weight of the legislative authority requires that it should be thus divided, the weakness of the executive may require, on the other hand, that it should be fortified. An absolute negative on the legislature appears, at first view, to be the natural defense with which the executive magistrate should be armed. But perhaps it would be neither altogether safe nor alone sufficient. On ordinary occasions it might not be exerted with the requisite firmness, and on extraordinary occasions it might be perfidiously abused. May not this defect of an absolute negative be supplied by some qualified connection between this weaker department and the weaker branch of the stronger department, by which the latter may be led to support the constitutional rights of the former, without being too much detached from the rights of its own department?

If the principles on which these observations are founded be just, as I persuade myself they are, and they be applied as a criterion to the several State constitutions, and to the federal Constitution it will be found that if the latter does not perfectly correspond with them, the former are infinitely less able to bear such a test.

There are, moreover, two considerations particularly applicable to the federal system of America, which place that system in a very interesting point of view.

First. In a single republic, all the power surrendered by the people is submitted to the administration of a single government; and the usurpations are guarded against by a division of the government into distinct and separate departments. In the compound republic of America, the power surrendered by the people is first divided between two distinct governments, and then the portion allotted to each subdivided among distinct and separate departments. Hence a double security arises to the rights of the people. The different governments will control each other, at the same time that each will be controlled by itself.

Second. It is of great importance in a republic not only to guard the society against the oppression of its rulers, but to guard one part of the society against the injustice of the other part. Different interests necessarily exist in different classes of citizens. If a majority be united by a common interest, the rights of the minority will be insecure. There are but two methods of providing against this evil: the one by creating a will in the community independent of the majority that is, of the society itself; the other, by comprehending in the society so many separate descriptions of citizens as will render an unjust combination of a majority of the whole very improbable, if not impracticable. The first method prevails in all governments possessing an hereditary or self-appointed authority. This, at best, is but a precarious security; because a power independent of the society may as well espouse the unjust views of the major, as the rightful interests of the minor party, and may possibly be turned against both parties. The second method will be exemplified in the federal republic of the United States. Whilst all authority in it will be derived from and dependent on the society, the society itself will be broken into so many parts, interests, and classes of citizens, that the rights of individuals, or of the minority, will be in little danger from interested combinations of the majority. In a free government the security for civil rights must be the same as that for religious rights. It consists in the one case in the multiplicity of interests, and in the other in the multiplicity of sects. The degree of security in both cases will depend on the number of interests and sects; and this may be presumed to depend on the extent of country and number of people comprehended under the same government. This view of the subject must particularly recommend a proper federal system to all the sincere and considerate friends of republican government, since it shows that in exact proportion as the territory of the Union may be formed into more circumscribed Confederacies, or States oppressive combinations of a majority will be facilitated: the best security, under the republican forms, for the rights of every class of citizens, will be diminished: and consequently the stability and independence of some member of the government, the only other security, must be proportionately increased. Justice is the end of government. It is the end of civil society. It ever has been and ever will be pursued until it be obtained, or until liberty be lost in the pursuit. In a society under the forms of which the stronger faction can readily unite and oppress the weaker, anarchy may as truly be said to reign as in a state of nature, where the weaker individual is not secured against the violence of the stronger; and as, in the latter state, even the stronger individuals are prompted, by the uncertainty of their condition, to submit to a government which may protect the weak as well as themselves; so, in the former state, will the more powerful factions or parties be gradually induced, by a like motive, to wish for a government which will protect all parties, the weaker as well as the more powerful. It can be little doubted that if the State of Rhode Island was separated from the Confederacy and left to itself, the insecurity of rights under the popular form of government within such narrow limits would be displayed by such reiterated oppressions of factious majorities that some power altogether independent of the people would soon be called for by the voice of the very factions whose misrule had proved the necessity of it. In the extended republic of the United States, and among the great variety of interests, parties, and sects which it embraces, a coalition of a majority of the whole society could seldom take place on any other principles than those of justice and the general good; whilst there being thus less danger to a minor from the will of a major party, there must be less pretext, also, to provide for the security of the former, by introducing into the government a will not dependent on the latter, or, in other words, a will independent of the society itself. It is no less certain than it is important, notwithstanding the contrary opinions which have been entertained, that the larger the society, provided it lie within a practical sphere, the more duly capable it will be of self-government. And happily for the republican cause, the practicable sphere may be carried to a very great extent, by a judicious modification and mixture of the federal principle.

Publius

 # Appendix E

Marbury v. Madison (1803)

Chief Justice Marshall delivered the opinion of the Court:

At the last term on the affidavits then read and filed with the clerk, a rule was granted in this case, requiring the Secretary of State to show cause why a mandamus should not issue, directing him to deliver to William Marbury his commission as a justice of the peace for the county of Washington, in the district of Columbia.

No cause has been shown, and the present motion is for a mandamus. The peculiar delicacy of this case, the novelty of some of its circumstances, and the real difficulty attending the points which occur in it, require a complete exposition of the principles on which the opinion to be given by the court is founded. . . .

In the order in which the court has viewed this subject, the following questions have been considered and decided:

1st. Has the applicant a right to the commission he demands?

2d. If he has a right, and that right has been violated, do the laws of his country afford him a remedy?

3d. If they do afford him a remedy, is it a mandamus issuing from this court?

The first object of inquiry is—1st. Has the applicant a right to the commission he demands? . . .

It [is] decidedly the opinion of the court, that when a commission has been signed by the president, the appointment is made; and that the commission is complete, when the seal of the United States has been affixed to it by the secretary of state. . . .

To withhold his commission, therefore, is an act deemed by the court not warranted by law, but violative of a vested legal right.

This brings us to the second inquiry; which is secondly: If he has a right, and that right has been violated, do the laws of his country afford him a remedy?

The very essence of civil liberty certainly consists in the right of every individual to claim the protection of the laws, whenever he receives an injury. One of the first duties of government is to afford that protection. [The] government of the United States has been emphatically termed a government of laws, and not of men. It will certainly cease to deserve this high appellation, if the laws furnish no remedy for the violation of a vested legal right. . . .

By the constitution of the United States, the President is invested with certain important political powers, in the exercise of which he is to use his own discretion, and is accountable only to his country in his political character, and to his own conscience. To aid him in the performance of these duties, he is authorized to appoint certain officers, who act by his authority and in conformity with his orders.

In such cases, their acts are his acts; and whatever opinion may be entertained of the manner in which executive discretion may be used, still there exists, and can exist, no power to control that discretion. The subjects are political. They respect the nation, not individual rights, and being entrusted to the executive, the decision of the executive is conclusive. . . .

But when the legislature proceeds to impose on that officer other duties; when he is directed peremptorily to perform certain acts; when the rights of individuals are dependent on the performance of those acts; he is so far the officer of the law; is amenable to the laws for his conduct; and cannot at his discretion sport away the vested rights of others.

The conclusion from this reasoning is, that where the heads of departments are the political or confidential agents of the executive, merely to execute the will of the President, or rather to act in cases in which the executive possesses a constitutional or legal discretion, nothing can be more perfectly clear than that their acts are only politically examinable. But where a specific duty is assigned by law, and individual rights depend upon the performance of that duty, it seems equally clear, that the individual who considers himself injured, has a right to resort to the laws of his country for a remedy. . . .

It is, then, the opinion of the Court [that Marbury has a] right to the commission; a refusal to deliver which is a plain violation of that right, for which the laws of his country afford him a remedy.

It remains to be enquired whether,

Thirdly. He is entitled to the remedy for which he applies. This depends on—First. The nature of the writ applied for, and,

   Secondly. The power of this court.

   First. The nature of the writ. . . .

This, then, is a plain case for a mandamus, either to deliver the commission, or a copy of it from the record; and it only remains to be enquired,

Whether it can issue from this court.

The act to establish the judicial courts of the United States authorizes the Supreme Court "to issue writs of mandamus in cases warranted by the principles and usages of law, to any courts appointed, or persons holding office, under the authority of the United States."

The Secretary of State, being a person holding an office under the authority of the United States, is precisely within the letter of the description; and if this court is not authorized to issue a writ of mandamus to such an officer, it must be because the law is unconstitutional, and therefore incapable of conferring the authority, and assigning the duties which its words purport to confer and assign.

The constitution vests the whole judicial power of the United States in one Supreme Court, and such inferior courts as congress shall, from time to time, ordain and establish. This power is expressly extended to all cases arising under the laws of the United States; and, consequently, in some form, may be exercised over the present case; because the right claimed is given by a law of the United States.

In the distribution of this power it is declared that "the Supreme Court shall have original jurisdiction in all cases affecting ambassadors, other public ministers and consuls, and those in which a state shall be a party. In all other cases, the Supreme Court shall have appellate jurisdiction."

It has been insisted, at the bar, that as the original grant of jurisdiction, to the supreme and inferior courts, is general, and the clause, assigning original jurisdiction to the Supreme Court, contains no negative or restrictive words, the power remains to the legislature, to assign original jurisdiction to that court in other cases than those specified in the article which has been recited; provided those cases belong to the judicial power of the United States.

If it had been intended to leave it in the discretion of the legislature to apportion the judicial power between the supreme and inferior courts according to the will of that body, it would certainly have been useless to have proceeded further than to have defined the judicial power, and the tribunals in which it should be vested. The subsequent part of the section is mere surplusage, is entirely without meaning, if such is to be the construction. If congress remains at liberty to give this court appellate jurisdiction, where the constitution has declared their jurisdiction shall be original; and original jurisdiction where the constitution has declared it shall be appellate; the distribution of jurisdiction, made in the constitution, is form without substance.

Affirmative words are often, in their operation, negative of other objects than those affirmed; and in this case, a negative or exclusive sense must be given to them or they have no operation at all.

It cannot be presumed that any clause in the constitution is intended to be without effect; and, therefore, such a construction is inadmissible, unless the words require it.

If the solicitude of the convention, respecting our peace with foreign powers, induced a provision that the supreme court should take original jurisdiction in cases which might be supposed to affect them; yet the clause would have proceeded no further than to provide for such cases, if no further restriction on the powers of congress had been intended. That they should have appellate jurisdiction in all other cases, with such exceptions as congress might make, is no restriction; unless the words be deemed exclusive of original jurisdiction.

When an instrument organizing fundamentally a judicial system, divides it into one supreme, and so many inferior courts as the legislature may ordain and establish; then enumerates its powers, and proceeds so far to distribute them, as to define the jurisdiction of the supreme court by declaring the cases in which it shall take original jurisdiction, and that in others it shall take appellate jurisdiction; the plain import of the words seems to be, that in one class of cases its jurisdiction is original, and not appellate; in the other it is appellate, and not original. If any other construction would render the clause inoperative, that is an additional reason for rejecting such other construction, and for adhering to their obvious meaning.

To enable this court, then, to issue a mandamus, it must be shown to be an exercise of appellate jurisdiction, or to be necessary to enable them to exercise appellate jurisdiction.

It has been stated at the bar that the appellate jurisdiction may be exercised in a variety of forms, and that if it be the will of the legislature that a mandamus should be used for that purpose, that will must be obeyed. This is true, yet the jurisdiction must be appellate, not original.

It is the essential criterion of appellate jurisdiction, that it revises and corrects the proceedings in a cause already instituted, and does not create that cause. Although, therefore, a mandamus may be directed to courts, yet to issue such a writ to an officer for the delivery of a paper, is in effect the same as to sustain an original action for that paper, and, therefore, seems not to belong to appellate, but to original jurisdiction. Neither is it necessary in such a case as this, to enable the court to exercise its appellate jurisdiction.

The authority, therefore, given to the Supreme Court, by the act establishing the judicial courts of the United States, to issue writs of mandamus to public officers, appears not to be warranted by the constitution; and it becomes necessary to enquire whether a jurisdiction, so conferred, can be exercised.

The question, whether an act, repugnant to the constitution, can become the law of the land, is a question deeply interesting to the United States; but happily, not of an intricacy proportioned to its interest. It seems only necessary to recognize certain principles, supposed to have been long and well established, to decide it.

That the people have an original right to establish, for their future government, such principles as, in their opinion, shall most conduce to their own happiness, is the basis on which the whole American fabric has been erected. The exercise of this original right is a very great exertion; nor can it, nor ought it, to be frequently repeated. The principles, therefore, so established, are deemed fundamental. And as the authority from which they proceed is supreme, and can seldom act, they are designed to be permanent.

This original and supreme will organizes the government, and assigns to different departments their respective powers. It may either stop here, or establish certain limits not to be transcended by those departments.

The government of the United States is of the latter description. The powers of the legislature are defined and limited; and that those limits may not be mistaken, or forgotten, the constitution is written. To what purpose are powers limited, and to what purpose is that limitation committed to writing, if these limits may, at any time, be passed by those intended to be restrained? The distinction between a government with limited and unlimited powers is abolished, if those limits do not confine the persons on whom they are imposed, and if acts prohibited and acts allowed, are of equal obligation. It is a proposition too plain to be contested, that the constitution controls any legislative act repugnant to it; or, that the legislature may alter the constitution by an ordinary act.

Between these alternatives there is no middle ground. The constitution is either a superior, paramount law, unchangeable by ordinary means, or it is on a level with ordinary legislative acts, and, like other acts, is alterable when the legislature shall please to alter it.

If the former part of the alternative be true, then a legislative act contrary to the constitution is not law: if the latter part be true, then written constitutions are absurd attempts, on the part of the people, to limit a power in its own nature illimitable.

Certainly all those who have framed written constitutions contemplate them as forming the fundamental and paramount law of the nation, and consequently, the theory of every such government must be, that an act of the legislature, repugnant to the constitution, is void.

This theory is essentially attached to a written constitution, and is, consequently, to be considered, by this court, as one of the fundamental principles of our society. It is not therefore to be lost sight of in the further consideration of this subject.

If an act of the legislature, repugnant to the constitution, is void, does it, notwithstanding its invalidity, bind the courts, and oblige them to give it effect? Or, in other words, though it be not law, does it constitute a rule as operative as if it was a law? This would be to overthrow in fact what was established in theory; and would seem, at first view, an absurdity too gross to be insisted on. It shall, however, receive a more attentive consideration.

It is emphatically the province and duty of the judicial department to say what the law is. Those who apply the rule to particular cases, must of necessity expound and interpret that rule. If two laws conflict with each other, the courts must decide on the operation of each.

So if a law be in opposition to the constitution; if both the law and the constitution apply to a particular case, so that the court must either decide that case conformably to the law, disregarding the constitution; or conformably to the constitution, disregarding the law; the court must determine which of these conflicting rules governs the case. This is of the very essence of judicial duty.

If, then, the courts are to regard the constitution, and the constitution is superior to any ordinary act of the legislature, the constitution, and not such ordinary act, must govern the case to which they both apply.

Those then who controvert the principle that the constitution is to be considered, in court, as a paramount law, are reduced to the necessity of maintaining that the courts must close their eyes on the constitution, and see only the law.

This doctrine would subvert the very foundation of all written constitutions. It would declare that an act which, according to the principles and theory of our government, is entirely void, is yet, in practice, completely obligatory. It would declare that if the legislature shall do what is expressly forbidden, such act, notwithstanding the express prohibition, is in reality effectual. It would be giving to the legislature a practical and real omnipotence, with the same breath which professes to restrict their powers within narrow limits. It is prescribing limits, and declaring that those limits may be passed at pleasure.

That it thus reduces to nothing what we have deemed the greatest improvement on political institutions—a written constitution—would of itself be sufficient, in America, where written constitutions have been viewed with so much reverence, for rejecting the construction. But the peculiar expressions of the constitution of the United States furnish additional arguments in favour of its rejection.

The judicial power of the United States is extended to all cases arising under the constitution.

Could it be the intention of those who gave this power, to say that in using it the constitution should not be looked into? That a case arising under the constitution should be decided without examining the instrument under which it arises?

This is too extravagant to be maintained.

In some cases, then, the constitution must be looked into by the judges. And if they can open it at all, what part of it are they forbidden to read or to obey?

There are many other parts of the constitution which serve to illustrate this subject.

It is declared that "no tax or duty shall be laid on articles exported from any state." Suppose a duty on the export of cotton, of tobacco, or of flour; and a suit instituted to recover it. Ought judgment to be rendered in such a case? Ought the judges to close their eyes on the constitution, and only see the law?

The constitution declares that "no bill of attainder or ex post facto law shall be passed." If, however, such a bill should be passed, and a person should be prosecuted under it; must the court condemn to death those victims whom the constitution endeavors to preserve?

"No person," says the constitution, "shall be convicted of treason unless on the testimony of two witnesses to the same overt act, or on confession in open court."

Here the language of the constitution is addressed especially to the courts. It prescribes, directly for them, a rule of evidence not to be departed from. If the legislature should change that rule, and declare one witness, or a confession out of court, sufficient for conviction, must the constitutional principle yield to the legislative act?

From these, and many other selections which might be made, it is apparent, that the framers of the constitution contemplated that instrument as a rule for the government of courts, as well as of the legislature. Why otherwise does it direct the judges to take an oath to support it? This oath certainly applies, in an especial manner, to their conduct in their official character. How immoral to impose it on them, if they were to be used as the instruments, and the knowing instruments, for violating what they swear to support!

The oath of office, too, imposed by the legislature, is completely demonstrative of the legislative opinion on this subject. It is in these words: "I do solemnly swear that I will administer justice without respect to persons, and do equal right to the poor and to the rich; and that I will faithfully and impartially discharge all the duties incumbent on me as _____, according to the best of my abilities and understanding, agreeably to the constitution, and laws of the United States." Why does a Judge swear to discharge his duties agreeably the constitution of the United States, if that constitution forms no rule for his government? If it is closed upon him, and cannot be inspected by him?

If such be the real state of things, this is worse than solemn mockery. To prescribe, or to take this oath, becomes equally a crime.

It is also not entirely unworthy of observation that in declaring what shall be the supreme law of the land, the constitution itself is first mentioned; and not the laws of the United States generally, but those only which shall be made in pursuance of the constitution, have that rank.

Thus, the particular phraseology of the constitution of the United States confirms and strengthens the principle, supposed to be essential to all written constitutions, that a law repugnant to the constitution is void; and that courts, as well as other departments, are bound by that instrument.

The rule must be discharged.

Source: 1 Cranch 137 (1803).

# Appendix F

McCulloch v. Maryland (1819)

Excerpts from Chief Justice John Marshall's Opinion:

In the case now to be determined, the defendant, a sovereign State, denies the obligation of a law enacted by the legislature of the Union, and the plaintiff, on his part, contests the validity of an act which has been passed by the legislature of that State. The constitution of our country, in its most interesting and vital parts, is to be considered; the conflicting powers of the government of the Union and of its members, as marked in that constitution, are to be discussed; and an opinion given, which may essentially influence the great operations of the government. No tribunal can approach such a question without a deep sense of its importance, and of the awful responsibility involved in its decision. But it must be decided peacefully, or remain a source of hostile legislation, perhaps of hostility of a still more serious nature; and if it is to be so decided, by this tribunal alone can the decision be made. On the Supreme Court of the United States has the constitution of our country devolved this important duty.

The first question made in the cause is, has Congress power to incorporate a bank? . . .[Second,] [w]hether the State of Maryland may, without violating the constitution, tax that branch?

That the power of taxation is one of vital importance; that it is retained by the states; that it is not abridged by the grant of a similar power to the government of the Union; that it is to be concurrently exercised by the two governments-are truths which have never been denied.

But such is the paramount character of the Constitution that its capacity to withdraw any subject from the action of even this power is admitted. The states are expressly forbidden to lay any duties on imports or exports, except what may be absolutely necessary for executing their inspection laws. . . . The same paramount character would seem to restrain . . . a state from such other exercise of this power as is in its nature incompatible with, and repugnant to, the constitutional laws of the Union. A law absolutely repugnant to another, as entirely repeals that other as if express terms of repeal were used.

On this ground the counsel for the Bank place its claim to be exempted from the power of a state to tax its operations. There is no express provision for the case, but the claim has been sustained on a principle which so entirely pervades the Constitution, is so intermixed with the materials which compose it, so interwoven with its web, so blended with its texture, as to be incapable of being separated from it without rending it into shreds.

This great principle is that the Constitution, and laws made in pursuance thereof, are supreme; that they control the constitutions and laws of the respective states, and cannot be controlled by them. From this, which may be almost termed an axiom, other propositions are deduced as corollaries. . . . These are: 1. That a power to create implies a power to preserve. 2. That a power to destroy, if wielded by a different hand, is hostile to, and incompatible with, these powers to create an preserve. 3. That where this repugnancy exists, that authority which is supreme must control, not yield to that over which it is supreme. . . .

That the power to tax involves the power to destroy; that the power to destroy may defeat and render useless the power to create; that there is a plain repugnance in conferring on one government a power to control the constitutional measures of another . . . are propositions not to be denied. . . .

If we apply the principle for which the state of Maryland contends, to the Constitution generally, we shall find it capable of changing totally the character of that instrument. We shall find it capable of arresting all the measures of the government, and of prostrating it at the foot of the states. The American people have declared their Constitution, and the laws made in pursuance thereof, to be supreme; and this principle would transfer the supremacy, in fact, to the states.

If the states may tax one instrument employed by the government in the execution of its powers, they may tax any and every other instrument. They may tax the mail; they may tax the mint; they may tax patent rights; they may tax the papers of the custom-house; they may tax judicial process; they may tax all the means employed by the government, to an excess which would defeat all the ends of government. This was not intended by the American people. They did not design to make their government dependent on the states. . . .

The question is, in truth, a question of supremacy. And if the right of the states to tax the means employed by the general government be conceded, the declaration that the Constitution, and the laws made in pursuance thereof, shall be the supreme law of the land, is empty and unmeaning declamation.

From 4 Wheaton 316, (430–433, 436, 437).

 # Appendix G

Barron v. Mayor & City Council of Baltimore (1833)

On Writ of Error to the Court of Appeals for the
Western Shore of the State of Maryland

Mr. Chief Justice Marshall delivered the opinion of the court.

The judgment brought up by this writ of error having been rendered by the court of a State, this tribunal can exercise no jurisdiction over it unless it be shown to come within the provisions of the 25th section of the Judiciary Act. The plaintiff in error contends that it comes within that clause in the Fifth Amendment to the Constitution which inhibits the taking of private property for public use without just compensation. He insists that this amendment, being in favor of the liberty of the citizen, ought to be so construed as to restrain the legislative power of a state, as well as that of the United States. If this proposition be untrue, the court can take no jurisdiction of the cause.

The question thus presented is, we think, of great importance, but not of much difficulty. The Constitution was ordained and established by the people of the United States for themselves, for their own government, and not for the government of the individual States. Each State established a constitution for itself, and in that constitution provided such limitations and restrictions on the powers of its particular government as its judgment dictated. The people of the United States framed such a government for the United States as they supposed best adapted to their situation and best calculated to promote their interests. The powers they conferred on this government were to be exercised by itself, and the limitations on power, if expressed in general terms, are naturally, and we think necessarily, applicable to the government created by the instrument. They are limitations of power granted in the instrument itself, not of distinct governments framed by different persons and for different purposes.

If these propositions be correct, the fifth amendment must be understood as restraining the power of the General Government, not as applicable to the States. In their several Constitutions, they have imposed such restrictions on their respective governments, as their own wisdom suggested, such as they deemed most proper for themselves. It is a subject on which they judge exclusively, and with which others interfere no further than they are supposed to have a common interest.

The counsel for the plaintiff in error insists that the Constitution was intended to secure the people of the several States against the undue exercise of power by their respective State governments, as well as against that which might be attempted by their General Government. In support of this argument he relies on the inhibitions contained in the tenth section of the first article. We think that section affords a strong, if not a conclusive, argument in support of the opinion already indicated by the court. The preceding section contains restrictions which are obviously intended for the exclusive purpose of restraining the exercise of power by the departments of the General Government. Some of them use language applicable only to Congress, others are expressed in general terms. The third clause, for example, declares, that "no bill of attainder or ex post facto law shall be passed." No language can be more general, yet the demonstration is complete that it applies solely to the Government of the United States. In addition to the general arguments furnished by the instrument itself, some of which have been already suggested, the succeeding section, the avowed purpose of which is to restrain State legislation, contains in terms the very prohibition. It declares, that "no State shall pass any bill of attainder or ex post facto law." This provision, then, of the ninth section, however comprehensive its language, contains no restriction on State legislation.

The ninth section having enumerated, in the nature of a bill of rights, the limitations intended to be imposed on the powers of the General Government, the tenth proceeds to enumerate those which were to operate on the State legislatures. These restrictions are brought together in the same section, and are by express words applied to the States. "No State shall enter into any treaty," etc. ... Perceiving, that in a constitution framed by the people of the United States, for the government of all, no limitation of the action of government on the people would apply to the State government, unless expressed in terms, the restrictions contained in the tenth section are in direct words so applied to the States.

It is worthy of remark, too, that these inhibitions generally restrain State legislation on subjects intrusted to the General Government, or in which the people of all the States feel an interest. A State is forbidden to enter into any treaty, alliance or confederation. If these compacts are with foreign nations, they interfere with the treaty-making power, which is conferred entirely on the General Government; if with each other, for political purposes, they can scarcely fail to interfere with the general purpose and intent of the Constitution. To grant letters of marque and reprisal, would lead directly to war, the power of declaring which is expressly given to Congress. To coin money is also the exercise of a power conferred on Congress. It would be tedious to recapitulate the several limitations on the powers of the States which are contained in this section. They will be found generally to restrain State legislation on subjects intrusted to the government of the Union, in which the citizens of all the States are interested. In these alone were the whole people concerned. The question of their application to States is not left to construction. It is averred in positive words.

If the original Constitution, in the ninth and tenth sections of the first article, draws this plain and marked line of discrimination between the limitations it imposes on the powers of the General Government and on those of the State; if, in every inhibition intended to act on State power, words are employed which directly express that intent; some strong reason must be assigned for departing from this safe and judicious course in framing the amendments before that departure can be assumed. We search in vain for that reason.

Had the people of the several States, or any of them, required changes in their Constitutions, had they required additional safeguards to liberty from the apprehended encroachments of their particular governments, the remedy was in their own hands, and could have been applied by themselves. A convention could have been assembled by the discontented State, and the required improvements could have been made by itself. The unwieldy and cumbrous machinery of procuring a recommendation from two-thirds of Congress and the assent of three-fourths of their sister States could never have occurred to any human being as a mode of doing that which might be effected by the State itself. Had the framers of these amendments intended them to be limitations on the powers of the State governments, they would have imitated the framers of the original Constitution, and have expressed that intention. Had Congress engaged in the extraordinary occupation of improving the Constitutions of the several States by affording the people additional protection from the exercise of power by their own governments in matters which concerned themselves alone, they would have declared this purpose in plain and intelligible language.

But it is universally understood, it is a part of the history of the day, that the great revolution which established the Constitution of the United States was not effected without immense opposition. Serious fears were extensively entertained that those powers which the patriot statesmen who then watched over the interests of our country deemed essential to union, and to the attainment of those invaluable objects for which union was sought, might be exercised in a manner dangerous to liberty. In almost every convention by which the Constitution was adopted, amendments to guard against the abuse of power were recommended. These amendments demanded security against the apprehended encroachments of the General Government—not against those of the local governments. In compliance with a sentiment thus generally expressed, to quiet fears thus extensively entertained, amendments were proposed by the required majority in Congress and adopted by the States. These amendments contain no expression indicating an intention to apply them to the State governments. This court cannot so apply them.

We are of opinion that the provision in the Fifth Amendment to the Constitution declaring that private property shall not be taken for public use without just compensation is intended solely as a limitation on the exercise of power by the Government of the United States, and is not applicable to the legislation of the States. We are therefore of opinion that there is no repugnancy between the several acts of the general assembly of Maryland, given in evidence by the defendants at the trial of this cause, in the court of that State, and the Constitution of the United States. This court, therefore, has no jurisdiction of the cause, and it is dismissed.

This cause came on to be heard on the transcript of the record from the Court of Appeals for the Western Shore of the State of Maryland, and was argued by counsel. On consideration whereof, it is the opinion of this Court that there is no repugnancy between the several acts of the General Assembly of Maryland given in evidence by the defendants at the trial of this cause in the court of that State and the Constitution of the United States; whereupon it is ordered and adjudged by this court that this writ of error be, and the same is hereby, dismissed for the want of jurisdiction.

 # Appendix H

The Gettysburg Address

Delivered on the battlefield at Gettysburg, Pennsylvania,
on November 19, 1863

Four score and seven years ago our fathers brought forth on this continent a new nation, conceived in liberty and dedicated to the proposition that all men are created equal. Now we are engaged in a great civil war, testing whether that nation or any nation so conceived and so dedicated can long endure. We are met on a great battlefield of that war. We have come to dedicate a portion of that field as a final resting-place for those who here gave their lives that that nation might live. It is altogether fitting and proper that we should do this. But in a larger sense, we cannot dedicate, we cannot consecrate, we cannot hallow this ground. The brave men, living and dead who struggled here have consecrated it far above our poor power to add or detract. The world will little note nor long remember what we say here, but it can never forget what they did here. It is for us the living rather to be dedicated here to the unfinished work which they who fought here have thus far so nobly advanced. It is rather for us to be here dedicated to the great task remaining before us—that from these honored dead we take increased devotion to that cause for which they gave the last full measure of devotion—that we here highly resolve that these dead shall not have died in vain, that this nation under God shall have a new birth of freedom, and that government of the people, by the people, for the people shall not perish from the earth.

Abraham Lincoln

 # Appendix I

Plessy v. Ferguson, (1896)

This case turns upon the constitutionality of an act of the general assembly of the state of Louisiana, passed in 1890, providing for separate railway carriages for the white and colored races. Acts 1890, No. 111, p. 152.

The first section of the statute enacts 'that all railway companies carrying passengers in their coaches in this state, shall provide equal but separate accommodations for the white, and colored races, by providing two or more passenger coaches for each passenger train, or by dividing the passenger coaches by a partition so as to secure separate accommodations: provided, that this section shall not be construed to apply to street railroads. No person or persons shall be permitted to occupy seats in coaches, other than the ones assigned to them, on account of the race they belong to.'

By the second section it was enacted 'that the officers of such passenger trains shall have power and are hereby required to assign each passenger to the coach or compartment used for the race to which such passenger belongs; any passenger insisting on going into a coach or compartment to which by race he does not belong, shall be liable to a fine of twenty-five dollars, or in lieu thereof to imprisonment for a period of not more than twenty days in the parish prison, and any officer of any railroad insisting on assigning a passenger to a coach or compartment other than the one set aside for the race to which said passenger belongs, shall be liable to a fine of twenty-five dollars, or in lieu thereof to imprisonment for a period of not more than twenty days in the parish prison; and should any passenger refuse to occupy the coach or compartment to which he or she is assigned by the officer of such railway, said officer shall have power to refuse to carry such passenger on his train, and for such refusal neither he nor the railway company which he represents shall be liable for damages in any of the courts of this state.'

The third section provides penalties for the refusal or neglect of the officers, directors, conductors, and employees of railway companies to comply with the act, with a proviso that 'nothing in this act shall be construed as applying to nurses attending children of the other race.' The fourth section is immaterial.

The information filed in the criminal district court charged, in substance, that Plessy, being a passenger between two stations within the state of Louisiana, was assigned by officers of the company to the coach used for the race to which he belonged, but he insisted upon going into a coach used by the race to which he did not belong. Neither in the information nor plea was his particular race or color averred.

The petition for the writ of prohibition averred that petitioner was seven-eights Caucasian and one-eighth African blood; that the mixture of colored blood was not discernible in him; and that he was entitled to every right, privilege, and immunity secured to citizens of the United States of the white race; and that, upon such theory, he took possession of a vacant seat in a coach where passengers of the white race were accommodated, and was ordered by the conductor to vacate said coach, and take a seat in another, assigned to persons of the colored race, and, having refused to comply with such demand, he was forcibly ejected, with the aid of a police officer, and imprisoned in the parish jail to answer a charge of having violated the above act.

The constitutionality of this act is attacked upon the ground that it conflicts both with the thirteenth amendment of the constitution, abolishing slavery, and the fourteenth amendment, which prohibits certain restrictive legislation on the part of the states.

1) That it does not conflict with the thirteenth amendment, which abolished slavery and involuntary servitude, except a punishment for crime, is too clear for argument. Slavery implies involuntary servitude,—a state of bondage; the ownership of mankind as a chattel, or, at least, the control of the labor and services of one man for the benefit of another, and the absence of a legal right to the disposal of his own person, property, and services. This amendment was said in the Slaughter-House Cases, 16 Wall. 36, to have been intended primarily to abolish slavery, as it had been previously known in this country, and that it equally forbade Mexican peonage or the Chinese coolie trade, when they amounted to slavery or involuntary servitude, and that the use of the word 'servitude' was intended to prohibit the use of all forms of involuntary slavery, of whatever class or name. It was intimated, however, in that case, that this amendment was regarded by the statesmen of that day as insufficient to protect the colored race from certain laws which had been enacted in the Southern states, imposing upon the colored race onerous disabilities and burdens, and curtailing their rights in the pursuit of life, liberty, and property to such an extent that their freedom was of little value; and that the fourteenth amendment was devised to meet this exigency.

So, too, in the Civil Rights Cases, 109 U.S. 3 , 3 Sup. Ct. 18, it was said that the act of a mere individual, the owner of an inn, a public conveyance or place of amusement, refusing accommodations to colored people, cannot be justly regarded as imposing any badge of slavery or servitude upon the applicant, but only as involving an ordinary civil injury, properly cognizable by the laws of the state, and presumably subject to redress by those laws until the contrary appears. 'It would be running the slavery question into the ground,' said Mr. Justice Bradley, 'to make it apply to every act of discrimination which a person may see fit to make as to the guests he will entertain, or as to the people he will take into his coach or cab or car, or admit to his concert or theater, or deal with in other matters of intercourse or business.'

A statute which implies merely a legal distinction between the white and colored races-a distinction which is founded in the color of the two races, and which must always exist so long as white men are distinguished from the other race by color-has no tendency to destroy the legal equality of the two races, or re-establish a state of involuntary servitude. Indeed, we do not understand that the thirteenth amendment is strenuously relied upon by the plaintiff in error in this connection.

2) By the fourteenth amendment, all persons born or naturalized in the United States, and subject to the jurisdiction thereof, are made citizens of the United States and of the state wherein they reside; and the states are forbidden from making or enforcing any law which shall abridge the privileges or immunities of citizens of the United States, or shall deprive any person of life, liberty, or property without due process of law, or deny to any person within their jurisdiction the equal protection of the laws.

The proper construction of this amendment was first called to the attention of this court in the Slaughter-House Cases, 16 Wall. 36, which involved, however, not a question of race, but one of exclusive privileges. The case did not call for any expression of opinion as to the exact rights it was intended to secure to the colored race, but it was said generally that its main purpose was to establish the citizenship of the negro, to give definitions of citizenship of the United States and of the states, and to protect from the hostile legislation of the states the privileges and immunities of citizens of the United States, as distinguished from those of citizens of the states. The object of the amendment was undoubtedly to enforce the absolute equality of the two races before the law, but, in the nature of things, it could not have been intended to abolish distinctions based upon color, or to enforce social, as distinguished from political, equality, or a commingling of the two races upon terms unsatisfactory to either. Laws permitting, and even requiring, their separation, in places where they are liable to be brought into contact, do not necessarily imply the inferiority of either race to the other, and have been generally, if not universally, recognized as within the competency of the state legislatures in the exercise of their police power. The most common instance of this is connected with the establishment of separate schools for white and colored children, which have been held to be a valid exercise of the legislative power even by courts of states where the political rights of the colored race have been longest and most earnestly enforced. . . .

Upon the other hand, where a statute of Louisiana required those engaged in the transportation of passengers among the states to give to all persons traveling within that state, upon vessels employed in that business, equal rights and privileges in all parts of the vessel, without distinction on account of race or color, and subjected to an action for damages the owner of such a vessel who excluded colored passengers on account of their color from the cabin set aside by him for the use of whites, it was held to be, so far as it applied to interstate commerce, unconstitutional and void. Hall v. De Cuir, 95 U.S. 485. The court in this case, however, expressly disclaimed that it had anything whatever to do with the statute as a regulation of internal commerce, or affecting anything else than commerce among the states.

In the Civil Rights Cases, 109 U.S. 3, 3 Sup. Ct. 18, it was held that an act of congress entitling all persons within the jurisdiction of the United States to the full and equal enjoyment of the accommodations, advantages, facilities, and privileges of inns, public conveyances, on land or water, theaters, and other places of public amusement, and made applicable to citizens of every race and color, regardless of any previous condition of servitude, was unconstitutional and void, upon the ground that the fourteenth amendment was prohibitory upon the states only, and the legislation authorized to be adopted by congress for enforcing it was not direct legislation on matters respecting which the states were prohibited from making or enforcing certain laws, or doing certain acts, but was corrective legislation, such as might be necessary or proper for counteracting and redressing the effect of such laws or acts. In delivering the opinion of the court, Mr. Justice Bradley observed that the fourteenth amendment 'does not invest congress with power to legislate upon subjects that are within the domain of state legislation, but to provide modes of relief against state legislation or state action of the kind referred to. It does not authorize congress to create a code of municipal law for the regulation of private rights, but to provide modes of redress against the operation of state laws, and the action of state officers, executive or judicial, when these are subversive of the fundamental rights specified in the amendment. Positive rights and privileges are undoubtedly secured by the fourteenth amendment; but they are secured by way of prohibition against state laws and state proceedings affecting those rights and privileges, and by power given to congress to legislate for the purpose of carrying such prohibition into effect; and such legislation must necessarily be predicated upon such supposed state laws or state proceedings, and be directed to the correction of their operation and effect.'. . .

While we think the enforced separation of the races, as applied to the internal commerce of the state, neither abridges the privileges or immunities of the colored man, deprives him of his property without due process of law, nor denies him the equal protection of the laws, within the meaning of the fourteenth amendment, we are not prepared to say that the conductor, in assigning passengers to the coaches according to their race, does not act at his peril, or that the provision of the second section of the act that denies to the passenger compensation in damages for a refusal to receive him into the coach in which he properly belongs is a valid exercise of the legislative power. Indeed, we understand it to be conceded by the state's attorney that such part of the act as exempts from liability the railway company and its officers is unconstitutional. The power to assign to a particular coach obviously implies the power to determine to which race the passenger belongs, as well as the power to determine who, under the laws of the particular state, is to be deemed a white, and who a colored, person. This question, though indicated in the brief of the plaintiff in error, does not properly arise upon the record in this case, since the only issue made is as to the unconstitutionality of the act, so far as it requires the railway to provide separate accommodations, and the conductor to assign passengers according to their race.

It is claimed by the plaintiff in error that, in an mixed community, the reputation of belonging to the dominant race, in this instance the white race, is 'property,' in the same sense that a right of action or of inheritance is property. Conceding this to be so, for the purposes of this case, we are unable to see how this statute deprives him of, or in any way affects his right to, such property. If he be a white man, and assigned to a colored coach, he may have his action for damages against the company for being deprived of his so-called 'property.' Upon the other hand, if he be a colored man, and be so assigned, he has been deprived of no property, since he is not lawfully entitled to the reputation of being a white man.

In this connection, it is also suggested by the learned counsel for the plaintiff in error that the same argument that will justify the state legislature in requiring railways to provide separate accommodations for the two races will also authorize them to require separate cars to be provided for people whose hair is of a certain color, or who are aliens, or who belong to certain nationalities, or to enact laws requiring colored people to walk upon one side of the street, and white people upon the other, or requiring white men's houses to be painted white, and colored men's black, or their vehicles or business signs to be of different colors, upon the theory that one side of the street is as good as the other, or that a house or vehicle of one color is as good as one of another color. The reply to all this is that every exercise of the police power must be reasonable, and extend only to such laws as are enacted in good faith for the promotion of the public good, and not for the annoyance or oppression of a particular class. Thus, in Yick Wo v. Hopkins, 118 U.S. 356, 6 Sup. Ct. 1064, it was held by this court that a municipal ordinance of the city of San Francisco, to regulate the carrying on of public laundries within the limits of the municipality, violated the provisions of the constitution of the United States, if it conferred upon the municipal authorities arbitrary power, at their own will, and without regard to discretion, in the legal sense of the term, to give or withhold consent as to persons or places, without regard to the competency of the persons applying or the propriety of the places selected for the carrying on of the business. It was held to be a covert attempt on the part of the municipality to make an arbitrary and unjust discrimination against the Chinese race. While this was the case of a municipal ordinance, a like principle has been held to apply to acts of a state legislature passed in the exercise of the police power. . . .

So far, then, as a conflict with the fourteenth amendment is concerned, the case reduces itself to the question whether the statute of Louisiana is a reasonable regulation, and with respect to this there must necessarily be a large discretion on the part of the legislature. In determining the question of reasonableness, it is at liberty to act with reference to the established usages, customs, and traditions of the people, and with a view to the promotion of their comfort, and the preservation of the public peace and good order. Gauged by this standard, we cannot say that a law which authorizes or even requires the separation of the two races in public conveyances is unreasonable, or more obnoxious to the fourteenth amendment than the acts of congress requiring separate schools for colored children in the District of Columbia, the constitutionality of which does not seem to have been questioned, or the corresponding acts of state legislatures.

We consider the underlying fallacy of the plaintiff's argument to consist in the assumption that the enforced separation of the two races stamps the colored race with a badge of inferiority. If this be so, it is not by reason of anything found in the act, but solely because the colored race chooses to put that construction upon it. The argument necessarily assumes that if, as has been more than once the case, and is not unlikely to be so again, the colored race should become the dominant power in the state legislature, and should enact a law in precisely similar terms, it would thereby relegate the white race to an inferior position. We imagine that the white race, at least, would not acquiesce in this assumption. The argument also assumes that social prejudices may be overcome by legislation, and that equal rights cannot be secured to the negro except by an enforced commingling of the two races. We cannot accept this proposition. If the two races are to meet upon terms of social equality, it must be the result of natural affinities, a mutual appreciation of each other's merits, and a voluntary consent of individuals. As was said by the court of appeals of New York in People v. Gallagher, 93 N. Y. 438, 448: 'This end can neither be accomplished nor promoted by laws which conflict with the general sentiment of the community upon whom they are designed to operate. When the government, therefore, has secured to each of its citizens equal rights before the law, and equal opportunities for improvement and progress, it has accomplished the end for which it was organized, and performed all of the functions respecting social advantages with which it is endowed.' Legislation is powerless to eradicate racial instincts, or to abolish distinctions based upon physical differences, and the attempt to do so can only result in accentuating the difficulties of the present situation. If the civil and political rights of both races be equal, one cannot be inferior to the other civilly or politically. If one race be inferior to the other socially, the constitution of the United States cannot put them upon the same plane.

It is true that the question of the proportion of colored blood necessary to constitute a colored person, as distinguished from a white person, is one upon which there is a difference of opinion in the different states; some holding that any visible admixture of black blood stamps the person as belonging to the colored race, others, that it depends upon the preponderance of blood and still others, that the predominance of white blood must only be in the proportion of three-fourths. But these are questions to be determined under the laws of each state, and are not properly put in issue in this case. Under the allegations of his petition, it may undoubtedly become a question of importance whether, under the laws of Louisiana, the petitioner belongs to the white or colored race.

The judgment of the court below is therefore affirmed.

Justice Harlan's dissenting opinion In the case of Plessy v. Ferguson

By the Louisiana statute the validity of which is here involved, all railway companies (other than street-railroad companies) carry passengers in that state are required to have separate but equal accommodations for white and colored persons, 'by providing two or more passenger coaches for each passenger train, or by dividing the passenger coaches by a partition so as to secure separate accommodations.' Under this statute, no colored person is permitted to occupy a seat in a coach assigned to white persons; nor any white person to occupy a seat in a coach assigned to colored persons. The managers of the railroad are not allowed to exercise any discretion in the premises, but are required to assign each passenger to some coach or compartment set apart for the exclusive use of is race. If a passenger insists upon going into a coach or compartment not set apart for persons of his race, he is subject to be fined, or to be imprisoned in the parish jail. Penalties are prescribed for the refusal or neglect of the officers, directors, conductors, and employees of railroad companies to comply with the provisions of the act.

Only 'nurses attending children of the other race' are excepted from the operation of the statute. No exception is made of colored attendants traveling with adults. A white man is not permitted to have his colored servant with him in the same coach, even if his condition of health requires the constant personal assistance of such servant. If a colored maid insists upon riding in the same coach with a white woman whom she has been employed to serve, and who may need her personal attention while traveling, she is subject to be fined or imprisoned for such an exhibition of zeal in the discharge of duty.

While there may be in Louisiana persons of different races who are not citizens of the United States, the words in the act 'white and colored races' necessarily include all citizens of the United States of both races residing in that state. So that we have before us a state enactment that compels, under penalties, the separation of the two races in railroad passenger coaches, and makes it a crime for a citizen of either race to enter a coach that has been assigned to citizens of the other race.

Thus, the state regulates the use of a public highway by citizens of the United States solely upon the basis of race.

However apparent the injustice of such legislation may be, we have only to consider whether it is consistent with the constitution of the United States. . . .

In respect of civil rights, common to all citizens, the constitution of the United States does not, I think, permit any public authority to know the race of those entitled to be protected in the enjoyment of such rights. Every true man has pride of race, and under appropriate circumstances, when the rights of others, his equals before the law, are not to be affected, it is his privilege to express such pride and to take such action based upon it as to him seems proper. But I deny that any legislative body or judicial tribunal may have regard to the race of citizens when the civil rights of those citizens are involved. Indeed, such legislation as that here in question is inconsistent not only with that equality of rights which pertains to citizenship, national and state, but with the personal liberty enjoyed by every one within the United States.

The thirteenth amendment does not permit the withholding or the deprivation of any right necessarily inhering in freedom. It not only struck down the institution of slavery as previously existing in the United States, but it prevents the imposition of any burdens or disabilities that constitute badges of slavery or servitude. It decreed universal civil freedom in this country. This court has so adjudged. But, that amendment having been found inadequate to the protection of the rights of those who had been in slavery, it was followed by the fourteenth amendment, which added greatly to the dignity and glory of American citizenship, and to the security of personal liberty, by declaring that 'all persons born or naturalized in the United States, and subject to the jurisdiction thereof, are citizens of the United States and of the state wherein they reside,' and that 'no state shall make or enforce any law which shall abridge the privileges or immunities of citizens of the United States; nor shall any state deprive any person of life, liberty or property without due process of law, nor deny to any person within its jurisdiction the equal protection of the laws.' These two amendments, if enforced according to their true intent and meaning, will protect all the civil rights that pertain to freedom and citizenship. Finally, and to the end that no citizen should be denied, on account of his race, the privilege of participating in the political control of his country, it was declared by the fifteenth amendment that 'the right of citizens of the United States to vote shall not be denied or abridged by the United States or by any state on account of race, color or previous condition of servitude.'

These notable additions to the fundamental law were welcomed by the friends of liberty throughout the world. They removed the race line from our governmental systems. They had, as this court has said, a common purpose, namely, to secure 'to a race recently emancipated, a race that through many generations have been held in slavery, all the civil rights that the superior race enjoy.' They declared, in legal effect, this court has further said, 'that the law in the states shall be the same for the black as for the white; that all persons, whether colored or white, shall stand equal before the laws of the states; and in regard to the colored race, for whose protection the amendment was primarily designed, that no discrimination shall be made against them by law because of their color.' We also said: 'The words of the amendment, it is true, are prohibitory, but they contain a necessary implication of a positive immunity or right, most valuable to the colored race,—the right to exemption from unfriendly legislation against them distinctively as colored; exemption from legal discriminations, implying inferiority in civil society, lessening the security of their enjoyment of the rights which others enjoy; and discriminations which are steps towards reducing them to the condition of a subject race.' It was, consequently, adjudged that a state law that excluded citizens of the colored race from juries, because of their race, however well qualified in other respects to discharge the duties of jurymen, was repugnant to the fourteenth amendment. . . . At the present term, referring to the previous adjudications, this court declared that 'underlying all of those decisions is the principle that the constitution of the United States, in its present form, forbids, so far as civil and political rights are concerned, discrimination by the general government or the states against any citizen because of his race. All citizens are equal before the law.' . . .

The decisions referred to show the scope of the recent amendments of the constitution. They also show that it is not within the power of a state to prohibit colored citizens, because of their race, from participating as jurors in the administration of justice.

It was said in argument that the statute of Louisiana does not discriminate against either race, but prescribes a rule applicable alike to white and colored citizens. But this argument does not meet the difficulty. Every one knows that the statute in question had its origin in the purpose, not so much to exclude white persons from railroad cars occupied by blacks, as to exclude colored people from coaches occupied by or assigned to white persons. Railroad corporations of Louisiana did not make discrimination among whites in the matter of accommodation for travelers. The thing to accomplish was, under the guise of giving equal accommodation for whites and blacks, to compel the latter to keep to themselves while traveling in railroad passenger coaches. No one would be so wanting in candor as to assert the contrary. The fundamental objection, therefore, to the statute, is that it interferes with the personal freedom of citizens. 'Personal liberty,' it has been well said, 'consists in the power of locomotion, of changing situation, or removing one's person to whatsoever places one's own inclination may direct, without imprisonment or restraint, unless by due course of law.' If a white man and a black man choose to occupy the same public conveyance on a public highway, it is their right to do so; and no government, proceeding alone on grounds of race, can prevent it without infringing the personal liberty of each.

It is one thing for railroad carriers to furnish, or to be required by law to furnish, equal accommodations for all whom they are under a legal duty to carry. It is quite another thing for government to forbid citizens of the white and black races from traveling in the same public conveyance, and to punish officers of railroad companies for permitting persons of the two races to occupy the same passenger coach. If a state can prescribe, as a rule of civil conduct, that whites and blacks shall not travel as passengers in the same railroad coach, why may it not so regulate the use of the streets of its cities and towns as to compel white citizens to keep on one side of a street, and black citizens to keep on the other? Why may it not, upon like grounds, punish whites and blacks who ride together in street cars or in open vehicles on a public road or street? Why may it not require sheriffs to assign whites to one side of a court room, and blacks to the other? And why may it not also prohibit the commingling of the two races in the galleries of legislative halls or in public assemblages convened for the consideration of the political questions of the day? Further, if this statute of Louisiana is consistent with the personal liberty of citizens, why may not the state require the separation in railroad coaches of native and naturalized citizens of the United States, or of Protestants and Roman Catholics?

The answer given at the argument to these questions was that regulations of the kind they suggest would be unreasonable, and could not, therefore, stand before the law. Is it meant that the determination of questions of legislative power depends upon the inquiry whether the statute whose validity is questioned is, in the judgment of the courts, a reasonable one, taking all the circumstances into consideration? A statute may be unreasonable merely because a sound public policy forbade its enactment. But I do not understand that the courts have anything to do with the policy or expediency of legislation. A statute may be valid, and yet, upon grounds of public policy, may well be characterized as unreasonable. Mr. Sedgwick correctly states the rule when he says that, the legislative intention being clearly ascertained, 'the courts have no other duty to perform than to execute the legislative will, without any regard to their views as to the wisdom or justice of the particular enactment.' Sedg. St. & Const. Law, 324. There is a dangerous tendency in these latter days to enlarge the functions of the courts, by means of judicial interference with the will of the people as expressed by the legislature. Our institutions have the distinguishing characteristic that the three departments of government are co-ordinate and separate. Each must keep within the limits defined by the constitution. And the courts best discharge their duty by executing the will of the law-making power, constitutionally expressed, leaving the results of legislation to be dealt with by the people through their representatives. Statutes must always have a reasonable construction. Sometimes they are to be construed strictly, sometimes literally, in order to carry out the legislative will. But, however construed, the intent of the legislature is to be respected if the particular statute in question is valid, although the courts, looking at the public interests, may conceive the statute to be both unreasonable and impolitic. If the power exists to enact a statute, that ends the matter so far as the courts are concerned. The adjudged cases in which statutes have been held to be void, because unreasonable, are those in which the means employed by the legislature were not at all germane to the end to which the legislature was competent.

The white race deems itself to be the dominant race in this country. And so it is, in prestige, in achievements, in education, in wealth, and in power. So, I doubt not, it will continue to be for all time, if it remains true to its great heritage, and holds fast to the principles of constitutional liberty. But in view of the constitution, in the eye of the law, there is in this country no superior, dominant, ruling class of citizens. There is no caste here. Our constitution is color-blind, and neither knows nor tolerates classes among citizens. In respect of civil rights, all citizens are equal before the law. The humblest is the peer of the most powerful. The law regards man as man, and takes no account of his surroundings or of his color when his civil rights as guaranteed by the supreme law of the land are involved. It is therefore to be regretted that this high tribunal, the final expositor of the fundamental law of the land, has reached the conclusion that it is competent for a state to regulate the enjoyment by citizens of their civil rights solely upon the basis of race.

In my opinion, the judgment this day rendered will, in time, prove to be quite as pernicious as the decision made by this tribunal in the Dred Scott Case.

It was adjudged in that case that the descendants of Africans who were imported into this country, and sold as slaves, were not included nor intended to be included under the word 'citizens' in the constitution, and could not claim any of the rights and privileges which that instrument provided for and secured to citizens of the United States; that, at time of the adoption of the constitution, they were 'considered as a subordinate and inferior class of beings, who had been subjugated by the dominant race, and, whether emancipated or not, yet remained subject to their authority, and had no rights or privileges but such as those who held the power and the government might choose to grant them.' The recent amendments of the constitution, it was supposed, had eradicated these principles from our institutions. But it seems that we have yet, in some of the states, a dominant race,—a superior class of citizens,—which assumes to regulate the enjoyment of civil rights, common to all citizens, upon the basis of race. The present decision, it may well be apprehended, will not only stimulate aggressions, more or less brutal and irritating, upon the admitted rights of colored citizens, but will encourage the belief that it is possible, by means of state enactments, to defeat the beneficent purposes which the people of the United States had in view when they adopted the recent amendments of the constitution, by one of which the blacks of this country were made citizens of the United States and of the states in which they respectively reside, and whose privileges and immunities, as citizens, the states are forbidden to abridge. Sixty millions of whites are in no danger from the presence here of eight millions of blacks. The destinies of the two races, in this country, are indissolubly linked together, and the interests of both require that the common government of all shall not permit the seeds of race hate to be planted under the sanction of law. What can more certainly arouse race hate, what more certainly create and perpetuate a feeling of distrust between these races, than state enactments which, in fact, proceed on the ground that colored citizens are so inferior and degraded that they cannot be allowed to sit in public coaches occupied by white citizens? That, as all will admit, is the real meaning of such legislation as was enacted in Louisiana.

The sure guaranty of the peace and security of each race is the clear, distinct, unconditional recognition by our governments, national and state, of every right that inheres in civil freedom, and of the equality before the law of all citizens of the United States, without regard to race. State enactments regulating the enjoyment of civil rights upon the basis of race, and cunningly devised to defeat legitimate results of the war, under the pretense of recognizing equality of rights, can have no other result than to render permanent peace impossible, and to keep alive a conflict of races, the continuance of which must do harm to all concerned. This question is not met by the suggestion that social equality cannot exist between the white and black races in this country. That argument, if it can be properly regarded as one, is scarcely worthy of consideration; for social equality no more exists between two races when traveling in a passenger coach or a public highway than when members of the same races sit by each other in a street car or in the jury box, or stand or sit with each other in a political assembly, or when they use in common the streets of a city or town, or when they are in the same room for the purpose of having their names placed on the registry of voters, or when they approach the ballot box in order to exercise the high privilege of voting.

There is a race so different from our own that we do not permit those belonging to it to become citizens of the United States. Persons belonging to it are, with few exceptions, absolutely excluded from our country. I allude to the Chinese race. But, by the statute in question, a Chinaman can ride in the same passenger coach with white citizens of the United States, while citizens of the black race in Louisiana, many of whom, perhaps, risked their lives for the preservation of the Union, who are entitled, by law, to participate in the political control of the state and nation, who are not excluded, by law or by reason of their race, from public stations of any kind, and who have all the legal rights that belong to white citizens, are yet declared to be criminals, liable to imprisonment, if they ride in a public coach occupied by citizens of the white race. It is scarcely just to say that a colored citizen should not object to occupying a public coach assigned to his own race. He does not object, nor, perhaps, would he object to separate coaches for his race if his rights under the law were recognized. But he does object, and he ought never to cease objecting, that citizens of the white and black races can be adjudged criminals because they sit, or claim the right to sit, in the same public coach on a public highway. The arbitrary separation of citizens, on the basis of race, while they are on a public highway, is a badge of servitude wholly inconsistent with the civil freedom and the equality before the law established by the constitution. It cannot be justified upon any legal grounds.

If evils will result from the commingling of the two races upon public highways established for the benefit of all, they will be infinitely less than those that will surely come from state legislation regulating the enjoyment of civil rights upon the basis of race. We boast of the freedom enjoyed by our people above all other peoples. But it is difficult to reconcile that boast with a state of the law which, practically, puts the brand of servitude and degradation upon a large class of our fellow citizens,—our equals before the law. The thin disguise of 'equal' accommodations for passengers in railroad coaches will not mislead any one, nor atone for the wrong this day done.

The result of the whole matter is that while this court has frequently adjudged, and at the present term has recognized the doctrine, that a state cannot, consistently with the constitution of the United States, prevent white and black citizens, having the required qualifications for jury service, from sitting in the same jury box, it is now solemnly held that a state may prohibit white and black citizens from sitting in the same passenger coach on a public highway, or may require that they be separated by a 'partition' when in the same passenger coach. May it not now be reasonably expected that astute men of the dominant race, who affect to be disturbed at the possibility that the integrity of the white race may be corrupted, or that its supremacy will be imperiled, by contact on public highways with black people, will endeavor to procure statutes requiring white and black jurors to be separated in the jury box by a 'partition,' and that, upon retiring from the court room to consult as to their verdict, such partition, if it be a movable one, shall be taken to their consultation room, and set up in such way as to prevent black jurors from coming too close to their brother jurors of the white race. If the 'partition' used in the court room happens to be stationary, provision could be made for screens with openings through which jurors of the two races could confer as to their verdict without coming into personal contact with each other. I cannot see but that, according to the principles this day announced, such state legislation, although conceived in hostility to, and enacted for the purpose of humiliating, citizens of the United States of a particular race, would be held to be consistent with the constitution.

I do not deem it necessary to review the decisions of state courts to which reference was made in argument. Some, and the most important, of them, are wholly inapplicable, because rendered prior to the adoption of the last amendments of the constitution, when colored people had very few rights which the dominant race felt obliged to respect. Others were made at a time when public opinion, in many localities, was dominated by the institution of slavery; when it would not have been safe to do justice to the black man; and when, so far as the rights of blacks were concerned, race prejudice was, practically, the supreme law of the land. Those decisions cannot be guides in the era introduced by the recent amendments of the supreme law, which established universal civil freedom, gave citizenship to all born or naturalized in the United States, and residing ere, obliterated the race line from our systems of governments, national and state, and placed our free institutions upon the broad and sure foundation of the equality of all men before the law.

I am of opinion that the state of Louisiana is inconsistent with the personal liberty of citizens, white and black, in that state, and hostile to both the spirit and letter of the constitution of the United States. If laws of like character should be enacted in the several states of the Union, the effect would be in the highest degree mischievous. Slavery, as an institution tolerated by law, would, it is true, have disappeared from our country; but there would remain a power in the states, by sinister legislation, to interfere with the full enjoyment of the blessings of freedom, to regulate civil rights, common to all citizens, upon the basis of race, and to place in a condition of legal inferiority a large body of American citizens, now constituting a part of the political community, called the 'People of the United States,' for whom, and by whom through representatives, our government is administered. Such a system is inconsistent with the guaranty given by the constitution to each state of a republican form of government, and may be stricken down by congressional action, or by the courts in the discharge of their solemn duty to maintain the supreme law of the land, anything in the constitution or laws of any state to the contrary notwithstanding.

For the reason stated, I am constrained to withhold my assent from the opinion and judgment of the majority.

Appendix J

Brown v. Board of Education of Topeka, Kansas (1954)
Supreme Court of the United States

Argued December 9, 1952
Reargued December 8, 1953
Decided May 17, 1954

Appeal from the United States District Court for the District of Kansas

Mr. Chief Justice Warren delivered the opinion of the Court.

These cases come to us from the States of Kansas, South Carolina, Virginia, and Delaware. They are premised on different facts and different local conditions, but a common legal question justifies their consideration together in this consolidated opinion.

In each of the cases, minors of the Negro race, through their legal representatives, seek the aid of the courts in obtaining admission to the public schools of their community on a non-segregated basis. In each instance, they had been denied admission to schools attended by white children under laws requiring or permitting segregation according to race. This segregation was alleged to deprive the plaintiffs of the equal protection of the laws under the Fourteenth Amendment. In each of the cases other than the Delaware case, a three-judge federal district court denied relief to the plaintiffs on the so-called "separate butequal" doctrine announced by this Court in Plessy v. Ferguson, 163 U.S. 537. Under that doctrine, equality of treatment is accorded when the races are provided substantially equal facilities, even though these facilities be separate. In the Delaware case, the Supreme Court of Delaware adhered to that doctrine, but ordered that the plaintiffs be admitted to the white schools because of their superiority to the Negro schools.

The plaintiffs contend that segregated public schools are not "equal" and cannot be made "equal," and that hence they are deprived of the equal protection of the laws. Because of the obvious importance of the question presented, the Court took jurisdiction. Argument was heard in the 1952 Term, and reargument was heard this Term on certain questions propounded by the Court.

Reargument was largely devoted to the circumstances surrounding the adoption of the Fourteenth Amendment in 1868. It covered exhaustively consideration of the Amendment in Congress, ratification by the states, then-existing practices in racial segregation, and the views of proponents and opponents of the Amendment. This discussion and our own investigation convince us that, although these sources cast some light, it is not enough to resolve the problem with which we are faced. At best, they are inconclusive. The most avid proponents of the post-War Amendments undoubtedly intended them to remove all legal distinctions among "all persons born or naturalized in the United States." Their opponents, just as certainly, were antagonistic to both the letter and the spirit of the Amendments and wished them to have the most limited effect. What others in Congress and the state legislatures had in mind cannot be determined with any degree of certainty.

An additional reason for the inconclusive nature of the Amendment's history with respect to segregated schools is the status of public education at that time. In the South, the movement toward free common schools, supported by general taxation, had not yet taken hold. Education of white children was largely in the hands of private groups. Education of Negroes was almost nonexistent, and practically all of the race were illiterate. In fact, any education of Negroes was forbidden by law in some states. Today, in contrast, many Negroes have achieved outstanding success in the arts and sciences, as well as in the business and professional world. It is true that public school education at the time of the Amendment had advanced further in the North, but the effect of the Amendment on Northern States was generally ignored in the congressional debates. Even in the North, the conditions of public education did not approximate those existing today. The curriculum was usually rudimentary; ungraded schools were common in rural areas; the school term was but three months a year in many states, and compulsory school attendance was virtually unknown. As a consequence, it is not surprising that there should be so little in the history of the Fourteenth Amendment relating to its intended effect on public education.

In the first cases in this Court construing the Fourteenth Amendment, decided shortly after its adoption, the Court interpreted it as proscribing all state-imposed discriminations against the Negro race. The doctrine of "separate but equal" did not make its appearance in this Court until 1896 in the case of Plessy v. Ferguson, supra, involving not education but transportation. American courts have since labored with the doctrine for over half a century. In this Court, there have been six cases involving the "separate but equal" doctrine in the field of public education. . . . In none of these cases was it necessary to reexamine the doctrine to grant relief to the Negro plaintiff. And in Sweatt v. Painter, supra, the Court expressly reserved decision on the question whether Plessy v. Ferguson should be held inapplicable to public education.

In the instant cases, that question is directly presented. Here, unlike Sweatt v. Painter, there are findings below that the Negro and white schools involved have been equalized, or are being equalized, with respect to buildings, curricula, qualifications and salaries of teachers, and other "tangible" factors. Our decision, therefore, cannot turn on merely a comparison of these tangible factors in the Negro and white schools involved in each of the cases. We must look instead to the effect of segregation itself on public education.

In approaching this problem, we cannot turn the clock back to 1868, when the Amendment was adopted, or even to 1896, when Plessy v. Ferguson was written. We must consider public education in the light of its full development and its present place in American life throughout the Nation. Only in this way can it be determined if segregation in public schools deprives these plaintiffs of the equal protection of the laws.

Today, education is perhaps the most important function of state and local governments. Compulsory school attendance laws and the great expenditures for education both demonstrate our recognition of the importance of education to our democratic society. It is required in the performance of our most basic public responsibilities, even service in the armed forces. It is the very foundation of good citizenship. Today it is a principal instrument in awakening the child to cultural values, in preparing him for later professional training, and in helping him to adjust normally to his environment. In these days, it is doubtful that any child may reasonably be expected to succeed in life if he is denied the opportunity of an education. Such an opportunity, where the state has undertaken to provide it, is a right which must be made available to all on equal terms.

We come then to the question presented: Does segregation of children in public schools solely on the basis of race, even though the physical facilities and other "tangible" factors may be equal, deprive the children of the minority group of equal educational opportunities? We believe that it does.

In Sweatt v. Painter, supra, in finding that a segregated law school for Negroes could not provide them equal educational opportunities, this Court relied in large part on "those qualities which are incapable of objective measurement but which make for greatness in a law school." In McLaurin v. Oklahoma State Regents, supra, the Court, in requiring that a Negro admitted to a white graduate school be treated like all other students, again resorted to intangible considerations: ". . . his ability to study, to engage in discussions and exchange views with other students, and, in general, to learn his profession." Such considerations apply with added force to children in grade and high schools. To separate them from others of similar age and qualifications solely because of their race generates a feeling of inferiority as to their status in the community that may affect their hearts and minds in a way unlikely ever to be undone. The effect of this separation on their educational opportunities was well stated by a finding in the Kansas case by a court which nevertheless felt compelled to rule against the Negro plaintiffs:

Segregation of white and colored children in public schools has a detrimental effect upon the colored children. The impact is greater when it has the sanction of the law, for the policy of separating the races is usually interpreted as denoting the inferiority of the negro group. A sense of inferiority affects the motivation of a child to learn. Segregation with the sanction of law, therefore, has a tendency to [retard] the educational and mental development of negro children and to deprive them of some of the benefits they would receive in a racial[ly] integrated school system.

Whatever may have been the extent of psychological knowledge at the time of Plessy v. Ferguson, this finding is amply supported by modern authority. Any language in Plessy v. Ferguson contrary to this finding is rejected.

We conclude that, in the field of public education, the doctrine of "separate but equal" has no place. Separate educational facilities are inherently unequal. Therefore, we hold that the plaintiffs and others similarly situated for whom the actions have been brought are, by reason of the segregation complained of, deprived of the equal protection of the laws guaranteed by the Fourteenth Amendment. This disposition makes unnecessary any discussion whether such segregation also violates the Due Process Clause of the Fourteenth Amendment.

Because these are class actions, because of the wide applicability of this decision, and because of the great variety of local conditions, the formulation of decrees in these cases presents problems of considerable complexity. On reargument, the consideration of appropriate relief was necessarily subordinated to the primary question—the constitutionality of segregation in public education. We have now announced that such segregation is a denial of the equal protection of the laws. In order that we may have the full assistance of the parties in formulating decrees, the cases will be restored to the docket, and the parties are requested to present further argument on Questions 4 and 5 previously propounded by the Court for the reargument this Term. The Attorney General of the United States is again invited to participate. The Attorneys General of the states requiring or permitting segregation in public education will also be permitted to appear as amici curiae upon request to do so by September 15, 1954, and submission of briefs by October 1, 1954.

It is so ordered.

 # Appendix K

THE FOUR FREEDOMS

(Excerpt of "State of the Union Address" delivered by President Franklin Delano Roosevelt, on January 6, 1941 to the Congress of the United States)

Mr. Speaker, Members of the 77th Congress:

I address you, the members of this new Congress, at a moment unprecedented in the history of the union. I use the word "unprecedented" because at no previous time has American security been as seriously threatened from without as it is today. . . .

As men do not live by bread alone, they do not fight by armaments alone. Those who man our defenses and those behind them who build our defenses must have the stamina and the courage which come from unshakeable belief in the manner of life which they are defending. The mighty action that we are calling for cannot be based on a disregard of all the things worth fighting for.

The nation takes great satisfaction and much strength from the things which have been done to make its people conscious of their individual stake in the preservation of democratic life in America. Those things have toughened the fiber of our people, have renewed their faith and strengthened their devotion to the institutions we make ready to protect. Certainly this is no time for any of us to stop thinking about the social and economic problems which are the root cause of the social revolution which is today a supreme factor in the world. For there is nothing mysterious about the foundations of a healthy and strong democracy.

The basic things expected by our people of their political and economic systems are simple. They are:

Equality of opportunity for youth and for others.

Jobs for those who can work.

Security for those who need it.

The ending of special privilege for the few.

The preservation of civil liberties for all.

The enjoyment of the fruits of scientific progress in a wider and constantly rising standard of living.

These are the simple, the basic things that must never be lost sight of in the turmoil and unbelievable complexity of our modern world. The inner and abiding straight of our economic and political systems is dependent upon the degree to which they fulfill these expectations. Many subjects connected with our social economy call for immediate improvement. As examples:

We should bring more citizens under the coverage of old-age pensions and unemployment insurance.

We should widen the opportunities for adequate medical care.

We should plan a better system by which persons deserving or needing gainful employment may obtain it.

I have called for personal sacrifice, and I am assured of the willingness of almost all Americans to respond to that call. A part of the sacrifice means the payment of more money in taxes. In my budget message I will recommend that a greater portion of this great defense program be paid for from taxation than we are paying for today. No person should try, or be allowed to get rich out of the program, and the principle of tax payments in accordance with ability to pay should be constantly before our eyes to guide our legislation.

If the congress maintains these principles the voters, putting patriotism ahead pocketbooks, will give you their applause.

In the future days which we seek to make secure, we look forward to a world founded upon four essential human freedoms.

The first is freedom of speech and expression—everywhere in the world.

The second is freedom of every person to worship God in his own way—everywhere in the world.

The third is freedom from want, which, translated into world terms, means economic understandings which will secure to every nation a healthy peacetime life for its inhabitants—everywhere in the world.

The fourth is freedom from fear, which, translated into world terms, means a world-wide reduction of armaments to such a point and in such a thorough fashion that no nation will be in a position to commit an act of physical aggression against any neighbor—anywhere in the wold.

That is no vision of a distant millennium. It is a definite basis for a kind of world attainable in our own time and generation. That kind of world is the very antithesis of the so-called "new order" of tyranny which the dictators seek to create with the crash of a bomb.

To that new order we oppose the greater conception—the moral order. A good society is able to face schemes of world domination and foreign revolutions alike without fear. Since the beginning of our American history we have been engaged in change, in a perpetual, peaceful revolution, a revolution which goes on steadily, quietly, adjusting itself to changing conditions without the concentration camp or the quicklime in the ditch. The world order which we seek is the cooperation of free countries, working together in a friendly, civilized society.

This nation has placed its destiny in the hands, heads and hearts of its millions of free men and women, and its faith in freedom under the guidance of God. Freedom means the supremacy of human rights everywhere. Our support goes to those who struggle to gain those rights and keep them. Our strength is our unity of purpose.

To that high concept there can be no end save victory.

 # Appendix L

HOW DEMOCRATIC IS AMERICA?

Howard Zinn

To give a sensible answer to the question "How democratic is America?" I find it necessary to make three clarifying preliminary statements. First, I want to define "democracy," not conclusively, but operationally, so we can know what we are arguing about or at least what I am talking about. Second, I want to state what my criteria are for measuring the "how" in the question. And third, I think it necessary to issue a warning about how a certain source of bias (although not the only source) is likely to distort our judgments.

Our definition is crucial. This becomes clear if we note how relatively easy is the answer to our question when we define democracy as a set of formal institutions and let it go at that. If we describe as "democratic" a country that has a representative system of government, with universal suffrage, a bill of rights, and party competition for office, it becomes easy to answer the question "how" with the enthusiastic reply, "Very!"...

I propose a set of criteria for the description "democratic" which goes beyond formal political institutions, to the quality of life in the society (economic, social, psychological), beyond majority rule to a concern for minorities, and beyond national boundaries to a global view of what is meant by "the people," in that rough, but essentially correct view of democracy as "government of, by, and for the people."

Let me list these criteria quality, because I will go on to discuss them in some detail later:

1. To what extent can various people in the society participate in those decisions which affect their lives: decisions in the political process and decisions in the economic structure?

2. As a corollary of the above: do people have equal access to the information which they need to make important decisions?

149

3. Are the members of the society equally protected on matters of life and death—in the most literal sense of that phrase?

4. Is there equality before the law: police, courts, the judicial process—as well as equality with the law-enforcing institutions, so as to safeguard equally everyone's person, and his freedom from interference by others and by the government?

5. Is there equality in the distribution of available resources: those economic goods necessary for health, life, recreation, leisure, growth?

6. Is there equal access to education, to knowledge and training, so as to enable persons in the society to live their lives as fully as possible, to enlarge their range of possibilities?

7. Is there freedom of expression on all matters, and equally for all, to communicate with other members of the society?

8. Is there freedom for individuality in private life, in sexual relations, family relations, the right of privacy?

9. To minimize regulation: do education and the culture in general foster a spirit of cooperation and amity to sustain the above conditions?

10. As a final safety feature: is there opportunity to protest, to disobey the laws, when the foregoing objectives are being lost—as a way of restoring them? . . .

Two historical facts support my enlarged definition of democracy. One is that the industrialized Western societies have outgrown the original notions which accompanied their early development: that constitutional and procedural tests sufficed for the "democracy" that overthrew the old order; that democracy was quite adequately fulfilled by the Bill of Rights in England at the time of the Glorious Revolution, the Constitution of the United States, and the declaration of the Rights of Man in France. It came to be acknowledged that the rhetoric of these revolutions was not matched by their real achievements. In other words, the limitations of that "democracy" led to the reformist and radical movements that grew up in the West in the middle and late nineteenth century. The other historical note is that the new revolutions in our century, in Africa, Asia, Latin America, while rejecting either in whole or in part the earlier revolutions, profess a similar democratic aim, but with an even broader rhetoric. . . .

My second preliminary point is on standards. By this I mean that we can judge in several ways the fulfillment of these ten criteria I have listed. We can measure the present against the past, so that if we find that in [1995] we are doing better in these matters than we were doing in 1860 or 1910, the society will get a good grade for its "democracy." I would adjure such an approach because it supports complacency. With such a standard, Russians in 1910 could point with pride to how much progress they had made toward parliamentary democracy; as Russians in [1985] could point to their post-Stalin progress away from the gulag; as Americans could point in 1939 to how far they had come toward solving the problem of economic equality; as Americans in the South could point in 1950 to the progress of the southern [African-American]. Indeed, the American government [has given] military aid to brutal regimes in Latin America on the ground that a decrease in the murders by semiofficial death squads is a sign of progress.

Or, we could measure our democracy against other places in the world. Given the high incidence of tyranny in the world, polarization of wealth, and lack of freedom of expression, the United States, even with very serious defects, could declare itself successful. Again, the result is to let us all off easily; some of our most enthusiastic self-congratulation is based on such a standard.

On the other hand, we could measure our democracy against an ideal (even if admittedly unachievable) standard. I would argue for such an approach, because, in what may seem to some a paradox, the ideal standard is the pragmatic one; it affects what we *do*. To grade a student on the basis of an improvement over past performance is justifiable if the intention is to encourage someone discouraged about his ability. But if he is rather pompous about his superiority in relation to other students (and I suggest this is frequently true of Americans evaluating American "democracy"), and if in addition he is a medical student about to graduate into a world ridden with disease, it would be best to judge him by an ideal standard. That might spur him to an improvement fast enough to save lives. . . .

My third preliminary point is a caution based on the obvious fact that we make our appraisals through the prism of our own status in society. This is particularly important in assessing democracy, because if "democracy" refers to the condition of masses of people, and if we as the assessors belong to a number of elites, we will tend (and I am not declaring an inevitability, just warning of a tendency) to see the present situation in America more benignly than it deserves. To be more specific, if democracy requires a keen awareness of the condition of black people, of poor people, of young people, of that majority of the world who are not American—and we are white, prosperous, beyond draft age, and American—then we have a number of pressures tending to dull our sense of inequity. We are, if not doomed to err, likely to err on the side of complacency—and we should try to take this into account in making our judgments.

1. Participation in Decisions

We need to recognize first, that whatever decisions are made politically are made by representatives of one sort or another: state legislators, congressmen, senators, and other elected officials, governors and presidents; also by those appointed by elected officials, like Supreme Court justices. These are important decisions, affecting our lives, liberties, and ability to pursue happiness. Congress and the president decide on the tax structure, which affects the distribution of resources. They decide how to spend the monies received, whether or not we go to war; who serves in the armed forces; what behavior is considered a crime; which crimes are prosecuted and which are not. They decide what limitations there should be on our travel, or on our right to speak freely. They decide on the availability of education and health services.

If representation by its very nature is undemocratic, as I would argue, this is an important fact for our evaluation. Representative government is *closer* to democracy than monarchy, and for this reason it has been hailed as one of the great political advances of modern times; yet, it is only a step in the direction of democracy, at its best. It has certain inherent flaws—pointed out by Rousseau in the eighteenth century, Victor Considerant in the nineteenth century, Robert Michels in the beginning of the twentieth century, Hannah Arendt in our own time. No representative can adequately represent another's needs; the representative tends to become a member of a special elite; he has privileges which weaken his sense of concern at others' grievances; the passions of the troubled lose force (as Madison noted in *The Federalist 10*) as they are filtered through the representative system; the elected official develops an expertise which tends toward its own perpetuation. Leaders develop what Michels called "a mutual insurance contract" against the rest of society. . . .

If only radicals pointed to the inadequacy of the political processes in the United States, we might be suspicious. But established political scientists of a moderate bent talk quite bluntly of the limitations of the voting system in the United States. Robert Dahl, in *A Preface to Democratic Theory*, drawing on the voting studies of American political scientists, concludes that "political activity, at least in the United States, is positively associated to a significant extent with such variables as income, socio-economic status, and education." He says:

> By their propensity for political passivity the poor and uneducated disfranchise themselves. . . . Since they also have less access than the wealthy to the organizational, financial, and propaganda resources that weigh so heavily in campaigns, elections, legislative, and executive decisions, anything like equal control over government policy is triply barred to the members of Madison's unpropertied masses. They are barred by their relatively greater inactivity, by their relatively limited access to resources, and by Madison's nicely contrived system of constitutional checks.[1]

Dahl thinks that our society is essentially democratic, but this is because he expects very little. (His book was written in the 1950s, when lack of commotion in the society might well have persuaded him that no one else expected much more than he did.) Even if democracy were to be superficially defined as "majority rule," the United States would not fulfill that, according to Dahl, who says that "on matters of specific policy, the majority rarely rules."[2] After noting that "the election is the critical technique for insuring that governmental leaders will be relatively responsive to nonleaders," he goes on to say that "it is important to notice how little a national election tells us about the preferences of majorities. Strictly speaking, all an election reveals the first preferences of some citizens among the candidates standing for office."[3] About 45 percent of the potential voters in national elections, and about 60 percent of the voters in local elections do not vote, and this cannot be attributed. Dahl says, simply to indifference. And if, as Dahl points out, "in no large nation state can elections tell us much about the preferences of majorities and minorities," this is "even more true of the interelection period." . . .

Dahl goes on to assert that the election process and interelection activity "are crucial processes for insuring that political leaders will be *somewhat* responsive to the preferences of *some* ordinary citizens."[4] I submit (the emphasized words are mine) that if an admirer of democracy in America can say no more than this, democracy is not doing very well.

Dahl tells us the election process is one of "two fundamental methods of social control which, operating together, make governmental leaders so responsive to nonleaders that the distinction between democracy and dictatorship still makes sense." Since his description of the election process leaves that dubious, let's look at his second requirement for distinguishing democracy: "The other method of social control is continuous political competition among individuals, parties, or both." What it comes down to is "not minority rule but minorities rule."[5]

If it turns out that this—like the election process—also has little democratic content, we will not be left with very much difference—by Dahl's own admission—between "dictatorship" and the "democracy" practiced in the United States. Indeed, there is much evidence on this: the lack of democracy within the major political parties, the vastly disproportionate influence of wealthy groups over poorer ones (what consumers' group in 1983 could match the $1 million spent by the Natural Gas Supply Association to lobby, in fifteen key congressional districts, for full control of natural gas prices?);[6] the unrepresentative nature of the major lobbies (the wealthy doctors speaking for all through the AMA, the wealthy farmers speaking for the poorer ones through the American Farm Bureau Federation, the most affluent trade unions speaking for all workers). All of this, and more, supports the idea of a "decline of American pluralism" that Henry Kariel has written about. What Dahl's democracy comes down to is "the steady appeasement of relatively small groups."[7] If these relatively small groups turn out to be the aircraft industry far more than the aged, the space industry far more than the poor, the Pentagon far more than the college youth—what is left of democracy?

Sometimes the elitism of decision-making is defended (by Dahl and by others) on the ground that the elite is enacting decisions passively supported by the mass, whose tolerance is proof of an underlying consensus in society. But Murray Levin's studies in *The Alienated Voter* indicate how much nonparticipation in elections is a result of hopelessness rather than approval. And Robert Wiebe, a historian at Northwestern University, talks of "consensus" becoming a "new stereotype." He approaches the question historically.

> *Industrialization arrived so peacefully not because all Americans secretly shared the same values or implicitly willed its success hut because its millions of bitter enemies lacked the mentality and the means to organize an effective counterattack.*[8]

Wiebe's point is that the passivity of most Americans in the face of elitist decision-making has not been due to acquiescence but to the lack of resources for effective combat, as well as a gulf so wide between the haves and have-nots that there was no ground on which to dispute. Americans neither revolted violently nor reacted at the polls; instead they were subservient, or else worked out their hostilities in personal ways. . . .

Presidential nominations and elections are more democratic than monarchical rule or the procedures of totalitarian states, but they are far from some reasonable expectation of democracy. The two major parties have a monopoly of presidential power, taking turns in the White House. The candidates of minority parties don't have a chance. They do not have access to the financial backing of the major parties, and there is not the semblance of equal attention in the mass media; it is only the two major candidates who have free access to prime time on national television.

More important, both parties almost always agree on the fundamentals of domestic and foreign policy, despite the election-year rhetoric which attempts to find important differences. Both parties arranged for United States intervention in Vietnam in the 1950s and 1960s, and both, when public opinion changed, promised to get out (note the Humphrey-Nixon contest of 1968). In 1984, Democratic candidate Walter Mondale agreed with Republican candidate Ronald Reagan that the United States (which had ten thousand thermonuclear warheads) needed to continue increasing its arms budget, although he asked for a smaller increase than the Republicans. Such a position left Mondale unable to promise representatives of the black community (where unemployment was over 20 percent) that he would spend even a few billion dollars for a jobs program. Meanwhile, Democrats and Republicans in Congress were agreeing on a $297 billion arms bill for the 1985 fiscal year.[9]

With all the inadequacies of the representative system, it does not even operate in the field of foreign policy. In exactly those decisions which are the most vital—matters of war and peace, life and death—power rests in the hands of the president and a small group of advisers. We don't notice this when wars seem to have a large degree of justification (as World War II); we begin to notice it when we find ourselves in the midst of a particularly pointless war.

I have been talking so far about democracy in the political process. But there is another serious weakness that I will only mention here, although it is of enormous importance: the powerlessness of the American to participate in economic decision-making, which affects his life at every moment. As a consumer, that is, as the person whom the economy is presumably intended to serve, he has virtually nothing to say about what is produced for him. The corporations make what is profitable; the advertising industry persuades him to buy what the corporations produce.

He becomes the passive victim of the misallocation of resources, the production of dangerous commodities, the spoiling of his air, water, forests, beaches, cities.

2. Access to Information

Adequate information for the electorate is a precondition for any kind of action (whether electoral or demonstrative) to affect national policy. As for the voting process, Berelson, Lazarsfeld, and McPhee tell us (in their book, *Voting*) after extensive empirical research: "One persistent conclusion is that the public is not particularly well informed about the specific issues of the day." . . .

Furthermore, . . . there are certain issues which never even reach the public because they are decided behind the scenes. . . .

Consider the information available to voters on two major kinds of issues. One of them is the tax structure, so bewilderingly complex that the corporation, with its corps of accountants and financial experts, can prime itself for lobbying activities, while the average voter, hardly able to comprehend his own income tax, stand by helplessly as the president, the Office of Management and Budget, and the Congress decide the tax laws. The dominant influences are those of big business, which has the resources both to understand and to act.

Then there is foreign policy. The government leads the citizenry to believe it has special expertise which, if it could only be revealed. Would support its position against critics. At the same time, it hides the very information which would reveal its position to be indefensible. The mendacity of the government on the Bay of Pigs operation, the secret operations of the CIA in Iran, Indonesia, Guatemala, and other places, the with-holding of vital information about the Tonkin Gulf events are only a few examples of the way the average person becomes a victim of government deception.

When the United States invaded the tiny island of Grenada in the fall of 1983, no reporters were allowed to observe the invasion, and the American public had little opportunity to get independent verification of the reasons given by the government for the invasion. As a result, President Reagan could glibly tell the nation what even one of his own supporters, journalist George Will, admitted was a lie: that he was invading Grenada to protect the lives of American medical students on the island. He could also claim that documents found on the island indicated plans for a Cuban-Soviet takeover of Grenada; the documents showed no such thing.[10]

Furthermore, the distribution of information to the public is a function of power and wealth. The government itself can color the citizens' understanding of events by its control of news at the source: the presidential press conference, the "leak to the press," the White Papers, the teams of "truth experts" going around the country at the taxpayers' expense. As for private media, the large networks and mass-circulation magazines have the greatest access to the public mind. There is no "equal time" for critics of public policy. . . .

3. Equal Protection

Let us go now from the procedural to the substantive, indeed to the most substantive of questions: the right of all people to life itself. Here we find democracy in America tragically inadequate. The draft, which has been a part of American law since 1940 (when it passed by one vote) decides, in wartime, who lives and who dies. Not only Locke, one of the leading theorists of the democratic tradition, declared the ultimate right of any person to safeguard his own life when threatened by the government; Hobbes, often looked on as the foe of democratic thought, agreed. The draft violates this principle, because it compels young people to sacrifice their lives for any cause which the leaders of government deem just; further it discriminates against the poor, the uneducated, the young.

It is in connection with this most basic of rights—life itself, the first and most important of those substantive ends which democratic participation is designed to safeguard—that I would assert the need for a global view of democracy. One can at least conceive of a democratic decision for martial sacrifice by those ready to make the sacrifice; a "democratic" war is thus a theoretical possibility. But that presumption of democracy becomes obviously false at the first shot because then others are affected who did not decide. . . . Nations making decisions to slaughter their own sons are at least theoretically subject to internal check. The victims on the other side fall without any such chance. For the United States today, this failure of democracy is total; we have the capacity to destroy the world without giving it a chance to murmur a dissent; we did, in fact, destroy a part of southeast Asia on the basis of a unilateral decision made in Washington. There is no more pernicious manifestation of the lack of democracy in America than this single fact.

4. Equality Before the Law

Is there equality before the law? At every stage of the judicial process— facing the policeman, appearing in court, being freed on bond, being sentenced by the judge—the poor person is treated worse than the rich, the black treated worse than the white, the politically or personally odd character is treated worse than the orthodox. The details are given in the 1963 report of the Attorney General's Committee on Poverty and the Administration of Federal Criminal Justice. There a defendant's poverty is shown to affect his preliminary hearing, his right to bail the quality of his counsel. The evidence is plentiful in the daily newspapers, which inform us that [an African-American] boy fleeing the scene of a two-dollar theft may be shot and killed by a pursuing policeman, while a wealthy man who goes to South America after a million-dollar swindle, even if apprehended, need never fear a scratch. The wealthy price-fixer for General Motors, who costs consumers millions, will get ninety days in jail, the burglar of a liquor store will get five years. An African-American youth, or a bearded white youth poorly dressed, has much more chance of being clubbed by a policeman on the street than a well-dressed white man, given the fact that both respond with equal tartness to a question. . . .

Aside from inequality among citizens, there is inequality between the citizen and his government, when they face one another in a court of law. Take the matter of counsel: the well-trained government prosecutor faces the indigent's court-appointed counsel. Four of my students did a study of the City Court of Boston several years ago. They sat in the court for weeks, taking notes, and found that the average time spent by court-appointed counsel with his client, before arguing the case at the bench, was seven minutes.

5. Distribution of Resources

Democracy is devoid of meaning if it does not include equal access to the available resources of the society. In India, democracy might still mean poverty; in the United States, with a Gross National Product of [more than] $3 trillion a year, democracy should mean that every American, working a short work-week, has adequate food, clothing, shelter, health care, education for himself and his family—in short, the material resources necessary to enjoy life and freedom. Even if only 20 percent of the American population is desperately poor . . . in a country so rich, that is an inexcusable breach of the democratic principle. Even if there is a large, prosperous middle class, there is something grossly unfair in the wealthiest fifth of the population getting 40 percent of the nation's income, and the poorest fifth getting 5 percent (a ratio virtually unchanged from 1947 to [1995]). . . .[11]

Whether you are poor or rich determines the most fundamental facts about your life: whether you are cold in the winter while trying to sleep, whether you suffocate in the summer; whether you live among vermin or rats; whether the smells around you all day are sweet or foul; whether you have adequate medical care; whether you have good teeth; whether you can send your children to college; whether you can go on vacation or have to take an extra job at night; whether you can afford a divorce, or an abortion, or a wife, or another child. . . .

6. Access to Education

In a highly industrialized society, education is a crucial determinant of wealth, political power, social status, leisure, and the ability to work in one's chosen field. Educational resources in our society are not equitably distributed. Among high-school graduates of the same IQ levels, a far higher percentage of the well-to-do go on to college than the poor.[12] A mediocre student with money can always go to college. A mediocre student without money may not be able to go, even to a state college, because he may have to work to support his family. Furthermore, the educational resources in the schools—equipment, teachers, etc.—are far superior in the wealthy suburbs than in the poor sections of the city, whether white or black.

7. Freedom of Expression

Like money, freedom of expression is available to all in America, but in widely varying quantities. The First Amendment formally guarantees freedom of speech, press, assembly, and petition to all—but certain realities of wealth, power, and status stand in the way of the equal distribution of these rights. Anyone can stand on a street corner and talk to ten or a hundred people. But someone with the resources to buy loudspeaker equipment, go through the necessary red tape, and post a bond with the city may hold a meeting downtown and reach a thousand or five thousand people. A person or a corporation with $100,000 can buy time on television and reach 10 million people. A rich person simply has much more freedom of speech than a poor person. The government has much more freedom of expression than a private individual, because the president can command the airwaves when he wishes, and reach 60 million people in one night.

Freedom of the press also is guaranteed to all. But the student selling an underground newspaper on the street with a nude woman on the cover may be arrested by a policeman, while the airport newsstand selling Playboy and ten magazines like it will remain safe. Anyone with $10,000 can put out a newspaper to reach a few thousand people. Anyone with $10 million can buy a few newspapers that will reach a few million people. Anyone who is penniless had better have a loud voice; and then he might be arrested for disturbing the peace.

8. Freedom for Individuality

The right to live one's life, in privacy and freedom, in whatever way one wants, so long as others are not harmed, should be a sacred principle in a democracy. But there are hundreds of laws, varying from state to state, and sometimes joined by federal laws, which regulate the personal lives of people in this country: their marriages, their divorces, their sexual relations. Furthermore, both laws and court decisions protect policemen and the FBI in their use of secret devices which listen in on private conversations, or peer in on private conduct.

9. The Spirit of Cooperation

The maintenance of those substantive elements of democracy which I have just sketched, if dependent on a pervasive network of coercion, would cancel out much of the benefit of that democracy. Democracy needs rather to be sustained by a spirit in society, the tone and the values of the culture. I am speaking of something as elusive as a mood, alongside something as hard as law, both of which would have to substitute cooperation tinged with friendly competition for the fierce combat of our business culture. I am speaking of the underlying drive that keeps people going in the society. So long as that drive is for money and power, with no ceiling on either, so long as ruthlessness is built into the rules of the game, democracy does not have a chance. If there is one crucial cause in the failure of American democracy—not the only one, of course, but a fundamental one—it is the drive for corporate profit, and the overwhelming influence of money in every aspect of our daily lives. That is the uncontrolled libido of our society from which the rape of democratic values necessarily follows.

The manifestations are diverse and endless: the Kefauver hearings on the drug industry in 1961 disclosed that the drive for profit in that industry had led to incredible overpricing of drugs for consumers (700 percent markup, for instance, for tablets to arthritic patients) as well as bodily harm resulting from "the fact that they market so many of their failures."

It was disclosed in 1979 that Johns-Manville, the nation's largest asbestos manufacturer, had deliberately withheld from its workers X-ray results which showed they were developing cancel.[13] The careless disposition of toxic wastes throughout the country and the repeated accidents at nuclear plants were testimony to the concern for corporate profit over human life.

If these were isolated cases, reported and then eliminated, they could be dismissed as unfortunate blemishes on an otherwise healthy social body. But the major allocations of resources in our society are made on the basis of money profit rather than social use. . . .

... [N]ews items buttress what I have said. The oil that polluted California's beautiful beaches in the 1960s . . . was produced by a system in which the oil companies' hunger for profit has far more weight than the ordinary person's need to swim in clean water. This is not to be attributed to Republicanism overriding the concern for the little fellow of the Democratic Party. Profit is master whichever party is in power; it was the liberal Secretary of the Interior Stewart Udall who allowed the dangerous drilling to go on. . . .

In 1984, the suit of several thousand veterans against the Dow Chemical Company, claiming that they and their families had suffered terrible illnesses as a result of exposure in Vietnam to the poisonous chemical Agent Orange, was settled. The Dow corporation avoided the disclosures of thousands of documents in open court by agreeing to pay $180 million to the veterans. One thing seemed clear: the company had known that the defoliant used in Vietnam might be dangerous, but it held back the news, and blamed the government for ordering use of the chemical. The government itself, apparently wanting to shift blame to the corporation, declared publicly that Dow Chemical had been motivated in its actions by greed for profit.

10. Opportunity to Protest

The first two elements in my list for democracy—decision-making and information to help make them—are procedural. The next six are substantive, dealing with the consequences of such procedures on life, liberty, and the pursuit of happiness. My ninth point, the one I have just discussed, shows how the money motive of our society corrupts both procedures and their consequences by its existence and suggests we need a different motive as a fundamental requisite of a democratic society. The point I am about to discuss is an ultimate requisite for democracy, a safety feature if nothing else—neither procedures nor consequences nor motivation—works. It is the right of citizens to break through the impasse of a legal and cultural structure, which sustains inequality, greed, and murder, to initiate processes for change. I am speaking of civil disobedience, which is an essential safeguard even in a successful society, and which is an absolute necessity in a society which is not going well.

If the institutional structure itself bars any change but the most picayune and grievances are serious, it is silly to insist that change must be mediated through the processes of that legal structure. In such a situation, dramatic expressions of protest and challenge are necessary to help change ways of thinking, to build up political power for drastic change. A society that calls itself democratic (whether accurately or not) must, as its ultimate safeguard, allow such acts of disobedience. If the government prohibits them (as we must expect from a government committed to the existent) then the members of a society concerned with democracy must not only defend such acts, but encourage them. Somewhere near the root of democratic thought is the theory of popular sovereignty, declaring that government and laws are instruments for certain ends, and are not to be deified with absolute obedience; they must constantly be checked by the citizenry, and challenged, opposed, even overthrown, if they become threats to fundamental rights.

Any abstract assessment of *when* disobedience is justified is pointless. Proper conclusions depend on empirical evidence about how bad things are at the moment, and how adequate are the institutional mechanisms for correcting them. . . .

One of these is the matter of race. The intolerable position of the African-American, in both North and South, has traditionally been handled with a few muttered apologies and tokens of reform. Then the civil disobedience of militants in the South forced our attention on the most dramatic (southern) manifestations of racism in America. The massive African-American urban uprisings of 1967 and 1968 showed that nothing less than civil disobedience (for riots and uprisings go beyond that) could make the nation see that the race problem is an American—not a southern—problem and that it needs bold, revolutionary action.

As for poverty: it seems clear that the normal mechanisms of congressional pretense and presidential rhetoric are not going to change things very much. Acts of civil disobedience by the poor will be required, at the least, to make middle-class America take notice, to bring national decisions that begin to reallocate wealth.

The war in Vietnam showed that we could not depend on the normal processes of "law and order," of the election process, of letters to *The Times,* to stop a series of especially brutal acts against the Vietnamese and against our own sons. It took a nationwide storm of protest, including thousands of acts of civil disobedience (14,000 people were arrested in one day in 1971 in Washington, D.C.), to help bring the war to an end. The role of draft resistance in affecting Lyndon Johnson's 1968 decision not to escalate the war further is told in the Defense Department secret documents of that period. In the 1980s civil disobedience [continued,] with religious pacifists and others risking prison in order to protest the arms race and the plans for nuclear war.

The great danger for American democracy is not from the protesters. That democracy is too poorly realized for us to consider critics—even rebels as the chief problem. Its fulfillment requires us all, living in an ossified system which sustains too much killing and too much selfishness, to join the protest.

Notes

1. Robert A. Dahl, *A Preface to Democratic Theory* (Chicago: University of Chicago Press, 1963), p. 81.

2. *Ibid.,* p. 124.

3. *Ibid,* p. 125.

4. *Ibid,* p. 131.

5. *Ibid,* pp. 131–32.

6. Thomas B. Edsall, *The New Politics of Inequality* (New York: Norton, 1984), p. 112.

7. Dahl, *A Preface to Democratic Theory,* p. 146.

8. Robert Wiebe, "The Confinements of Consensus," *TriQuarterly,* 1966, Copyright by TriQuarterly 1966. All rights reserved.

9. *New York Times,* September 25, 1984.

10. The *New York Times* reported, November 5, 1983: "There is nothing in the documents, however, that specifically indicates that Cuba and the Soviet Union were on the verge of taking over Grenada, as Administration officials have suggested."

11. Edsall, The New Politics of Inequality, p. 221.

12. See the Carnegie Council on Children study, *Small Futures,* by Rich deLore, 1979.

13. *Los Angeles Times,* May 3, 1979.

How Democratic Is America?

A Response to Howard Zinn

Sidney Hooks

Charles Pierce, the great American philosopher, once observed that there was such a thing as the "ethics of words." The "ethics of words" are violated whenever ordinary terms are used in an unusual context or arbitrarily identified with another concept for which other terms are in common use. Mr. Zinn is guilty of a systematic violation of the "ethics of words." In consequence, his discussion of "democracy" results in a great many methodological errors as well as inconsistencies. To conserve space, I shall focus on three.

I

First of all, he confuses democracy as a political *process* with democracy as a political *product* or state of welfare; democracy as a "*free* society" with democracy as a "*good* society," where good is defined in terms of equality or justice (or both) or some other constellation of values. One of the reasons for choosing to live under a democratic political system rather than a nondemocratic system is our belief that it makes possible a better society. That is something that must be empirically established, something denied by critics of democracy from Plato to Santayana. The equality which is relevant to democracy as a *political process* is, in the first instance, political equality with respect to the rights of citizenship. Theoretically, a politically democratic community could vote, wisely or unwisely, to abolish, retain, or establish certain economic inequalities. Theoretically, a benevolent despotism could institute certain kinds of social and even juridical equalities. Historically, the Bismarckian political dictatorship introduced social welfare legislation for the masses at a time when such legislation would have been repudiated by the existing British and American political democracies. Some of Mr. Zinn's proposed reforms could be introduced under a dictatorship or benevolent despotism. Therefore, they are not logically or organically related to democracy.

The second error in Mr. Zinn's approach to democracy is "to measure our democracy against an ideal (even if inadvertently unachievable) standard . . . even if utopian. . ." without *defining* the standard. His criteria admittedly are neither necessary nor sufficient for determining the presence of democracy since he himself admits that they are applicable to societies that are not democratic. Further, even if we were to take his criteria as severally defining the presence of democracy—as we might take certain physical and mental traits as constituting a definition of health—he gives no operational test for determining whether or not they have been fulfilled. For example, among the criteria he lists for determining whether a society is democratic is this: "Are the members of the society equally protected on matters of life and death—in the most literal sense of that phrase?" A moment's reflection will show that here—as well as in other cases where Zinn speaks of equality—it is impossible for all members to be equally protected on matters of life and death—certainly not in a world in which men do the fighting and women give birth to children, where children need more protection than adults, and where some risk-seeking adults require and deserve less protection (since resources are not infinite) than others. As Karl Marx realized, "in the most literal sense that phrase," there cannot be absolute equality even in a classless society. . . .

The only sensible procedure in determining the absence or presence of equality from a democratic perspective is comparative. We must ask whether a culture is more or less democratic in comparison to the past with respect to some *desirable feature* of equality (Zinn ignores the fact that not all equalities are desirable). It is better for some people to be more intelligent and more knowledgeable than others than for all to be unintelligent and ignorant. There never is literally equal access to education, to knowledge and training in any society. The question is: Is there more access today for more people than yesterday, and how can we increase the access tomorrow?

Mr. Zinn refuses to take this approach because, he asserts, "it supports complacency." It does nothing of the sort! On the contrary, it shows that progress is possible, and encourages us to exert our efforts in the same direction if we regard the direction as desirable.

It will be instructive to look at the passage in which Mr. Zinn objects to this sensible comparative approach because it reveals the bias in his approach:

"With such a standard," he writes, "Russia in 1910 could point with pride to how much progress they had made toward parliamentary democracy; as Russians in 1985 could point to their post-Stalin progress away from the gulag; as Americans could point in 1939 to how far they had come in solving the problem of economic equality; as Americans in the South could point in 1950 to the progress of the southern African-American."

a) In 1910 the Russians were indeed moving toward greater progress in local parliamentary institutions. Far from making them complacent, they moved towards more inclusive representative institutions which culminated in elections to the Constituent Assembly in 1918, which was bayoneted out of existence by Lenin and the Communist Party, with a minority party dictatorship established.

b) Only Mr. Zinn would regard the slight diminution in terror from the days of Stalin to the regime of Chernenko as progress toward democracy. Those who observe the ethics of words would normally say that the screws of repression had been slightly relaxed. Mr. Zinn seems unaware that as bad as the terror was under Lenin, it was not as pervasive as it is today.* But no one with any respect for the ethics of words would speak of "the progress of democracy" in the Soviet Union from Lenin to Stalin to Khrushchev to Chernenko. Their regimes were varying degrees of dictatorship and terror.

c) Americans could justifiably say that in 1939 progress had been made in giving workers a greater role, not as Mr. Zinn says in "solving the problem of economic equality" (a meaningless phrase), but in determining the conditions and rewards of work that prevailed in 1929 or previously because the existence of the Wagner Labor Relations Act made collective bargaining the law of the land. They could say this not to rest in complacency, but to use the organized force of their trade unions to influence further the political life of the country. And indeed, it was the organized labor movement in 1984 which in effect chose the candidate of the Democratic Party.

d) Americans in the South in 1950 could right-fully speak of the progress of the southern African-American over the days of unrestricted Jim Crow and lynching bees of the past, *not* to rest in complacency, but to agitate for further progress through the Supreme Court decision of *Brown v. Board of Education in Topeka* and through the Civil Rights Act of Congress. This has not made them complacent, but more resolved to press further to eliminate remaining practices of invidious discrimination.

Even Mr. Zinn should admit that with respect to some of his other criteria this is the only sensible approach. Otherwise we get unhistorical answers, the hallmark of the doctrinaire. He asks—criterion 1—"To what extent can various people in the society participate in those decisions which affect their lives?" and—criterion 7—"Is there freedom of expression on all matters, and equally for all, to communicate with other members of the society?" Why doesn't Mr. Zinn adopt this sensible comparative approach? Because it would lead him to inquire into the extent to which people are free to participate in decisions that effect their lives *today*, free to express

---

*These words and subsequent references to the Soviet Union preceded the reforms initiated under Mikhail Gorbachev and continued with greater intensity under Boris Yeltsin—*Editors.*

themselves, free to organize, free to protest and dissent today, *in comparison with the past.* It would lead him to the judgment *which he wishes to avoid at all costs,* to wit, that despite the grave problems, gaps, and tasks before us, the United States is *more* democratic today than it was a hundred years ago, fifty years ago, twenty years ago, five years ago with respect to every one of the criteria he has listed. To recognize this is not an invitation to complacency. On the contrary, it indicates the possibility of broadening, deepening, and using the democratic political process to improve the quality of human life, to modify and redirect social institutions in order to realize on a wider scale the moral commitment of democracy to an equality of concern for all its citizens to achieve their fullest growth as persons. This commitment is to a process, not to a transcendent goal or a fixed, ideal standard.

In a halting, imperfect manner, set back by periods of violence, vigilantism, and xenophobia, the political democratic process in the United States has been used to modify the operation of the economic system. The improvements and reforms won from time to time make the still-existing problems and evils more acute in that people become more aware of them. The more the democratic process extends human freedoms, and the more it introduces justice in social relations and the distribution of wealth, the greater grows the desire for more freedom and justice. Historically and psychologically, it is false to assume that reforms freed a spirit of complacency. . . .

The third and perhaps most serious weakness in Mr. Zinn's view is his conception of the nature of the formal political democratic process. It suffers from several related defects. First, it overlooks the central importance of majority rule in the democratic process. Second, it denies in effect that majority rule is possible by defining democracy in such a way that it becomes impossible. . . .

"Representation by its very nature," claims Mr. Zinn, "is undemocratic." This is Rousseauistic nonsense. For it would mean that no democracy— including all societies that Mr. Zinn ever claimed at any time to be democratic—could possibly exist, not even the direct democracies or assemblies of Athens or the New England town meetings. For all such assemblies must elect officials to carry out their will. If no representative (and an official is a representative, too) can adequately represent another's needs, there is no assurance that in the actual details of governance, the selectmen, road commissioners, or other town or assembly officials will, in fact, carry out their directives. No assembly or meeting can sit in continuous session or collectively carry out the common decision. In the nature of the case, officials, like representatives, constitute an elite and their actions may reflect their interests more than the interests of the governed. This makes crucial the questions whether and how an elite can be removed, whether the consent on which the rule of the officials or representatives rests is free or coerced, whether a minority can peacefully use these mechanisms, by which freely given consent is registered, to win over or become a majority. The existence of representative assemblies makes democracy difficult, not impossible.

Since Mr. Zinn believes that a majority never has any authority to bind i minority as well as itself by decisions taken after free discussion and debate, he is logically committed to anarchy. Failing to see this, he confuses two fundamentally different things—the meaning or definition of democracy, and its justification.

1. A democratic government is one in which the general direction of policy rests directly or indirectly upon the freely given consent of a majority of the adults governed. Ambiguities and niceties aside, that is what democracy means. It is not anarchy. The absence of a unanimous consensus does not entail the absence of democracy.

2. One may reject on moral or religious or personal grounds a democratic society. Plato, as well as modern totalitarians, contends that a majority of mankind is either too stupid or vicious to be entrusted with self-government, or to be given the power to accept or reject their ruling elites, and that the only viable alternative to democracy is the self-selecting and self-perpetuating elite of "the wise," or "the efficient," or "the holy," or "the strong," depending upon the particular ideology of the totalitarian apologist. The only thing they have in common with democrats is their rejection of anarchy.

3. No intelligent and moral person can make an *absolute* of democracy in the sense that he believes it is always, everywhere, under any conditions, and no matter what its consequences, ethically legitimate. Democracy is obviously not desirable in a head-hunting or cannibalistic society or in an institution of the feeble-minded. But wherever and whenever a principled democrat accepts the political system of democracy, he must accept the binding authority of legislative decisions, reached after the free give-and-take of debate and discussion, as binding upon him whether he is a member of the majority or minority. Otherwise the consequence is incipient of overt anarchy or civil war, the usual preface to despotism or tyranny. Accepting the decision of the majority as binding does not mean that it is final or

irreversible. The processes of freely given consent must make it possible for a minority to urge amendment or repeal of any decision of the majority. Under carefully guarded provisions, a democrat may resort to civil disobedience of a properly enacted law in order to bear witness to the depths of his commitment in an effort to reeducate his fellow citizens. But in that case he must voluntarily accept punishment for his civil disobedience, and so long as he remains a democrat, voluntarily abandon his violation or noncompliance with law at the point where its consequences threaten to destroy the democratic process and open the floodgates either to the violent disorders of anarchy or to the dictatorship of a despot or a minority political party.

4. That Mr. Zinn is not a democrat but an anarchist in his views is apparent in his contention that not only must a democracy allow or tolerate civil disobedience within limits, but that "members of a society concerned with democracy must not only defend such acts, but encourage them." On this view, if southern segregationists resort to civil disobedience to negate the long-delayed but eminently just measures adopted by the government to implement the amendments that outlaw slavery, they should be encouraged to do so. On this view, any group that defies any law that violates its conscience—with respect to marriage, taxation, vaccination, abortion, education—should be encouraged to do so. Mr. Zinn, like most anarchists, refuses to generalize the principles behind his action. He fails to see that if all fanatics of causes deemed by them to be morally just were encouraged to resort to civil disobedience, even our imperfect existing political democracy would dissolve in chaos, and that civil disobedience would soon become quite uncivil. He fails to see that in a democracy the processes of intelligence, not individual conscience, must be supreme.

II

I turn now to some of the issues that Mr. Zinn declares are substantive. Before doing sol wish to make clear my belief that the most substantive issue of all is the procedural one by which the inescapable differences of interests among men, once a certain moral level of civilization has been reached, are to be negotiated. The belief in the validity of democratic procedures rests upon the conviction that where adult human beings have freedom of access to relevant information, they are, by and large, better judges of their own interests than are those who set themselves up as their betters and rulers, that, to use the homely maxim, those who wear the shoes know best where they pinch and therefore have the right to change their political shoes in the light of their experience. . . .

Looking at the question "How democratic is America?" with respect to the problems of poverty, race, education, etc., we must say "Not democratic enough!", but not for the reasons Mr. Zinn gives. For he seems to believe that the failure to adopt *his* solutions and proposals with respect to foreign policy, slum clearance, pollution, etc., is evidence of the failure of the democratic process itself. He overlooks the crucial difference between the procedural process and the substantive issues. When he writes that democracy is devoid of meaning if it does not include "equal access to the available resources of the society," he is simply abusing language. Assuming such equal access is desirable (which some might question who believe that access to some of society's resources—for example, to special-ized training or to scarce supplies—should go not equally to all but to the most needful or sometimes to the most qualified), a democracy may or may not legislate such equal access. The crucial question is whether the electorate has the power to make the choice, or to elect those who would carry out the mandate chosen. . . .

When Mr. Zinn goes on to say that "in the United States . . . democracy should mean that every American, working a short work-week, has ade-quate food, clothing, shelter, health care, . . ." he is not only abusing lan-guage, he is revealing the fact that the procedural processes that are essential to the meaning of democracy, in ordinary usage, are not essential to his conception. He is violating the basic ethics of discourse. If demo-cracy "should mean" what Zinn says it should, then were Huey Long or any other dictator to seize power and introduce a "short work-week" and distribute "adequate food, clothing, shelter, health care" to the masses, Mr. Zinn would have to regard his regime as democratic.

After all, when Hitler came to power and abolished free elections in Germany, he at the same time reduced unemployment, increased the real wages of the German worker, and provided more adequate food, clothing, shelter, and health care than was available under the Weimar Republic. On Zinn's view of what democracy "should mean," this made Hitler's rule more democratic than that of Weimar. . . .

Not surprisingly, Mr. Zinn is a very unreliable guide even in his account of the procedural features of the American political system. In one breath he maintains that not enough information is available to voters to make intelligent choices on major political issues like tax laws. (The voter, of course, does not vote on such laws but for representatives who have taken stands on a number of complete issues.) "The dominant influences are those of big business, which has the resources both to understand and to act." In another breath, he complains that the electorate is at the mercy of the propagandist. "The propagandist does not need to lie; he overwhelms the public with so much information as to lead it to believe that it is all too complicated for anyone but the experts."

Mr. Zinn is certainly hard to please! The American political process is not democratic because the electorate hasn't got enough information. It is also undemocratic because it receives too much information. What would Zinn have us do so that the public gets just the right amount of information and propaganda? Have the government control the press? Restrict freedom of propaganda? But these are precisely the devices of totalitarian societies. The evils of the press, even when it is free of government control, are many indeed. The great problem is to keep the press free and responsible. And as defective as the press and other public media are today surely it is an exaggeration to say that with respect to tax laws "the dominant influences are those of big business." If they were, how can we account for the existence of the income tax laws? If the influence of big business on the pres4i is so dominant and the press is so biased, how can we account for the fact that although 92 percent of the press opposed Truman's candidacy in 194X, he was reelected? How can we account for the profound dissatisfaction of Vice President Agnew with the press and other mass media?* And since Mr. Zinn believes that big business dominates our educational system, especially our universities, how can we account for the fact that the universities are the centers of the strongest dissent in the nation to public and national policy, that the National Association of Manufacturers bitterly complained a few years ago that the economics of the free enterprise system was derided, and often not even taught, in most Departments of Economics in the colleges and universities of the nation?

Mr. Zinn's exaggerations are really caricatures of complex realities. Far from being controlled by the monolithic American corporate economy, American public opinion is today marked by a greater scope and depth of dissent than at any time in its history, except for the days preceding the Civil War. The voice and the votes of Main Street still count for more in a democratic polity than those of Wall Street. Congress has limited, and can still further limit, the influence of money on the electoral process by federal subsidy and regulations. There are always abuses needing reforms. By failing to take a comparative approach and instead focusing on some

---

*Spiro Agnew, former governor of Maryland and vice president before being forced from office during the first term of Richard Nixon (1968–1972), was a frequent and vociferous critic of the "liberal" press—Editors.

absolute utopian standard of perfection, Mr. Zinn gives an exaggerated, tendentious, and fundamentally false picture of the United States. There is hardly a sentence in his essay that is free of some serious flaw in perspective, accuracy, or emphasis. Sometimes they have a comic effect, as when Mr. Zinn talks about the lack of "equal distribution of the right of freedom of expression." What kind of "equal distribution" is he talking about? Of course, a person with more money can talk to more people than one with less, although this does not mean that more persons will listen to him, agree with him, or be influenced by him. But a person with a more eloquent voice or a better brain can reach more people than you or 1. What shall we do to insure equal distribution of the right of freedom of expression? Insist on equality of voice volume or pattern, and equality of brain power? More money gives not only greater opportunity to talk to people than less money but the ability to do thousands of things barred to those who have less money. Shall we then decree that all people have the same amount of money all the time and forbid anyone from depriving anyone else of any of his money even by fair means? "The government," writes Mr. Zinn, "has much more freedom of expression than a private individual because the president can command the airwaves when he wishes, and reach 60 million people in one night."

Alas! Mr. Zinn is not joking. Either he wants to bar the president or any public official from using the airwaves or he wants all of us to take turns. One wonders what country Mr. Zinn is living in. Nixon spoke to 60 million people several times, and so did Jimmy Carter. What was the result? More significant than the fact that 60 million people hear the president is that 60 million or more can hear his critics, sometimes right after he speaks, and that no one is compelled to listen.

Mr. Zinn does not understand the basic meaning of equality in a free, open democratic society. Its philosophy does not presuppose that all citizens are physically or intellectually equal or that all are equally gifted in every or any respect. It holds that all enjoy a moral equality, and that therefore, as far as is practicable, given finite resources, the institutions of a democratic society should seek to provide an equal opportunity to all its citizens to develop themselves to their full desirable potential.

Of course, we cannot ever provide complete equal opportunity. More and more is enough. For one thing, so long as children have different parents and home environments, they cannot enjoy the same or equal opportunities. Nonetheless, the family has compensating advantages for all that. Let us hope that Mr. Zinn does not wish to wipe out the family to avoid differences in opportunity. Plato believed that the family, as we know it, should be abolished because it did not provide equality of opportunity, and that all children should be brought up by the state.

Belief in the moral equality of men and women does not require that all individuals be treated identically or that equal treatment must be measured or determined by equality of outcome or result. Every citizen should have an equal right to an education, but that does not mean that, regardless of capacity and interest, he or she should have the same amount of schooling beyond the adolescent years, and at the same schools, and take the same course of study. With the increase in nadonal wealth, a good case can be made for an equal right of all citizens to health care or medical treatment. But only a quack or ideological fanatic would insist that therefore all individuals should have the same medical regimen no matter what ails them. This would truly be putting all human beings in the bed of Procrustes.

This conception of moral equality as distinct from Mr. Zinn's notions of equality is perfectly compatible with intelligent recognition of human inequalities and relevant ways of treating their inequalities to further both the individual and common good. Intelligent and loving parents are equally concerned with the welfare of all their children. But precisely because they are, they may provide different specific strategies in health care, education, psychological motivation, and intellectual stimulation to develop the best in all of them. The logic of Mr. Zinn's position although he seems blissfully unaware of it—leads to the most degrading kind of egalitarian socialism, the kind which Marx and Engels in their early years denounced as "barracks socialism."

It is demonstrable that democracy is healthier and more effective where human beings do not suffer from poverty, unemployment, and disease. It is also demonstrable that to the extent that property gives power, private property in the means of social production gives power over the lives of those who must live by its use, and, therefore, that such property, whether public or private, should be responsible to those who are affected by its operation. Consequently one can argue that political democracy depends not only on the extension of the franchise to all adults, not only on its active exercise, but on programs of social welfare that provide for collective bargaining by free trade unions of workers and employees, unemployment insurance, minimum wages, guaranteed health care, and other social services that are integral to the welfare state. It is demonstrable that although the existing American welfare state provides far more welfare than was ever provided in the past—my own lifetime furnishes graphic evidence of the vast changes—it is still very far from being a genuine welfare state. Political democracy Call exist without a welfare state, but it is stronger and better with it.

The basic issue that divides Mr. Zinn from others no less concerned about human welfare, but less fanatical than he is how a genuine welfare state is to be brought about. My contention is that this can be achieved by the vigorous exercise of the existing democratic process, and that by the same coalition politics through which great gains have been achieved in the past, even greater gains can be won in the future.

For purposes of economy, I focus on the problem of poverty, or since this is a relative term, hunger. If the presence of hunger entails the absence of the democratic political process, then democracy has never existed in the past—which would be an arbitrary use of words. Nonetheless, the existence of hunger is always a threat to the continued existence of the democratic process because of the standing temptation of those who hunger to exchange freedom for the promise of bread. This, of course, is an additional ground to the even weightier moral reasons for gratifying basic human needs.

That fewer people go hungry today in the United States than ever before may show that our democracy is better than it used to be but not that it is as good as it can be. Even the existence of one hungry person is one too many. How then can hunger or the extremes of poverty be abolished? Certainly not by the method Mr. Zinn advises: "Acts of civil disobedience by the poor will be required, at the least, to make middle-class America take notice, to bring national decisions that begin to reallocate wealth."

This is not only a piece of foolish advice, it is dangerously foolish advice. Many national decisions to reallocate wealth have been made through the political process—what else is the system of taxation if not a method of reallocating wealth?—without resort to civil disobedience. Indeed, resort to civil disobedience on this issue is very likely to produce a backlash among those active and influential political groups in the community who are aware that normal political means are available for social and economic reform. The refusal to engage in such normal political processes could easily be exploited by demagogues to portray the movement towards the abolition of hunger and extreme poverty as a movement towards the confiscation and equalization of all wealth.

The simplest and most effective way of abolishing hunger is to act on the truly revolutionary principle, enunciated by the federal government, that it is responsible for maintaining a standard of relief as a minimum beneath which a family will not be permitted to sink. . . .

For reasons that need no elaboration here, the greatest of the problems faced by American democracy today is the race problem. Although tied to the problems of poverty and urban reconstruction, it has independent aspects exacerbated by the legacy of the Civil War and the Reconstruction period.

Next to the American Indians, African-Americans have suffered most from the failure of the democratic political process to extend the rights and privileges of citizenship to those whose labor and suffering have contributed so much to the conquest of the continent. The remarkable gains that have been made by African-Americans in the last twenty years have been made primarily through the political process. If the same rate of improvement continues, the year 2000 may see a rough equality established. The growth of African-American suffrage, especially in the South, the increasing by the white community, despite periodic setbacks resulting from outbursts of violence, opens up a perspective of continuous and cumulative reform. The man and the organization he headed chiefly responsible for the great gains made by African-Americans. Roy Wilkins and the NAACP, were convinced that the democratic political process can be more effectively used to further the integration of African-Americans into our national life than by reliance on any other method. . . .

The only statement in Mr. Zinn's essay that I can wholeheartedly endorse is his assertion that the great danger to Americans democracy does not come from the phenomena of protest as such. Dissent and protest are integral to the democratic process. The danger comes from certain modes of dissent, from the substitution of violence and threats of violence for the mechanisms of the political process, from the escalation of that violence as the best hope of those who still have grievances against our imperfect American democracy, and from views such as those expressed by Mr. Zinn which downgrade the possibility of peaceful social reform an encourage rebellion. It is safe to predict that large-scale violence will backfire, that they will create a climate of repression that may reverse the course of social progress and expanded civil liberties of the last generation. . . .

It is when Mr. Zinn is discussion racial problems that his writing ceases to be comic and silly and becomes irresponsible and mischievious. He writes:

> The massive African-American urban uprisings of 1967 and 1968 showed that nothing less than civil disobedience (for riots and uprisings go beyond that) could make the nation see that the race problem is an American—not a southern—problem and that it needs bold, revolutionary action.

First of all, every literate person knows that the race problem is an American problem, not exclusively a southern one. It needs no civil disobedience or "black uprisings" to remind us of that. Second, the massive uprisings of 1967 and 1968 were violent and uncivil, and resulted in needless loss of life and suffering. The Civil Rights Acts, according to Roy Wilkins, then head of the NAACP, were imperiled by them. They were adopted despite, not because, of them. Third, what kind of "revolutionary" action is Mr. Zinn calling for? And by whom? He seems to lack the courage of his confusions. Massive civil disobedience when sustained becomes a form of civil war.

Despite Mr. Zinn and others, violence is more likely to produce reaction than reform. In 1827 a resolution to manumit slaves by purchase (later, Lincoln's preferred solution) was defeated by three votes in the House of Burgesses of the State of Virginia. It was slated to be reintroduced in a subsequent session with excellent prospects of being adopted. Had Virginia adopted it, North Carolina would shortly have followed suit. But before it could be reintroduced, Nat Turner's rebellion broke out. Its violent excesses frightened the South into a complete rejection of a possibility that might have prevented the American Civil War—the fiercest and bloodiest war in human history up to that time, from whose consequences American society is still suffering. Mr. Zinn's intentions are as innocent as those of a child playing with matches.

III

One final word about "the global" dimension of democracy of which Mr. Zinn speaks. Here, too, he speaks sympathetically of actions that would undermine the willingness and capacity of a free society to resist totalitarian aggression.

The principles that should guide a free democratic society in a world where dictatorial regimes seek to impose their rule on other nations were formulated by John Stuart Mill, the great defender of liberty and representative government, more than a century ago:

> *To go to war for an idea, if the war is aggressive not defensive, is as criminal as to go to war for territory or revenue, for it is as little justifiable to force our ideas on other people, as to compel them to submit to our will in any other aspect. . . .* **The doctrine of non-intervention, to he a legitimate principle of morality, must be accepted by all governments.** *The despots must consent to he bound by it as well as the free states. Unless they do, the profession of it by free countries comes but to this miserable issue, that the wrong side may help the wrong side but the right may not help the right side. Intervention to*

enforce non-intervention is always right, always moral if not always prudent. *Though it may be a mistake to give freedom (or independence—S H.) to a people who do not value the boon, it cannot be right to insist that if they do value it, they shall not be hindered from the pursuit of it by foreign coercion* (Fraser's Magazine, 1859, emphasis mine).

Unfortunately, these principles were disregarded by the United States in 1936 when Hitler and Mussolini sent troops to Spain to help Franco overthrow the legally elected democratic Loyalist regime. The U.S. Congress, at the behest of the administration, adopted a Neutrality Resolution which prevented the democratic government of Spain from purchasing arms here. This compelled the Spanish government to make a deal with Stalin, who not only demanded its entire gold supply but the acceptance of the dread Soviet secret police, the NKVD, to supervise the operations. The main operation of the NKVD in Spain was to engage in a murderous purge of the democratic ranks of anti-Communists which led to the victory of Franco. The story is told in George Orwell's *Homage to Catalonia*. He was on the scene.

The prudence of American intervention in Vietnam may be debatable but there is little doubt that [UN ambassador] Adlai Stevenson, sometimes referred to as the liberal conscience of the nation, correctly stated the American motivation when he said at the UN on the very day of his death: "My hope in Vietnam is that resistance there may establish the fact that changes in Asia are not to be precipitated by outside force. This was the point of the Korean War. This is the point of the conflict in Vietnam."

. . . Mr. Zinn's remarks about Grenada show he is opposed to the liberal principles expressed by J. S. Mill in the passage cited above. His report of the facts about Grenada is as distorted as his account of present-day American democracy. On tiny Grenada, whose government was seized by Communist terrorists, were representatives of every Communist regime in the Kremlin's orbit, Cuban troops, and a Soviet general. I have read the documents captured by the American troops. They conclusively establish that the Communists were preparing the island as part of the Communist strategy of expansion.[1]

It is sad but significant that Mr. Zinn, whose heart bleeds for the poor Asians who suffered in the struggle to prevent the Communist takeover in Southeast Asia, has not a word of protest, not a tear of compassion for the hundreds of thousands of tortured, imprisoned, and drowned in flight after the victory of the North Vietnamese "liberators," not to mention the even greater number of victims of the Cambodian and Cuban Communists.

One summary question may be asked whose answer bears on the issue of how democratic America is. Suppose all the iron and bamboo and passport curtains of the world were lifted today, in what direction would freedom loving and democratic people move? Anyone is free to leave the United States today, except someone fleeing from the law, but in [some of] the countries arrayed against the United States people are penned in like animals and cannot cross a boundary without risking death. Has this no significance for the "global" aspect of our question?

Notes

1. *THE GRENADA PAPERS: The Inside Story of the Grenadian Revolution—and the Making of a Totalitarian State as Told in Captured Documents* (San Francisco: Institute of Contemporary Studies, 1984).

 # Appendix M

DOES GOVERNMENT DO WHAT PEOPLE WANT?

Kenneth Janda

Of course, even if the United States fits more closely to the pluralist than the majoritarian model of democracy, we nevertheless should expect the government to respond to public opinion. But does it? How often? And on what issues?

In assessing whether the U.S. government does what the people want, we rely heavily on two major studies. In one, Alan Monroe compared public opinion on public issues with government policy outcomes for 327 cases from 1960 through 1980. He first asked whether the public favored a change in policy on the issue or preferred the status quo. He then classified subsequent government action as manifesting a "change" or the "status quo." If the public favored a change, and government policy changed accordingly, the policy was judged to be *consistent* with public opinion. Similarly, if the public favored the status quo and government policy continued as before, the policy was also scored as consistent. Obviously, when government policy did not reflect public opinion, the case was counted as *inconsistent*.

Overall., Monroe found that government policy conformed to public opinion on 63 percent of all 327 cases. Although this may seem reassuring for majoritarian democracy, understand that about 50 percent of the cases would be consistent if government policy were decided purely by chance. More interesting, there were important differences in policy outcomes when the public favored a change instead of the status quo. As shown in Figure 1, government policy was far more likely (82 percent) to match public opinion if the people liked things as they were. If the public favored a policy change, government policy was almost as likely to remain the same as to change.

Janda et al., *The Challenge of Democracy*, Second Edition, Copyright © 1989 by Houghton Mifflin Company. Used with permission.

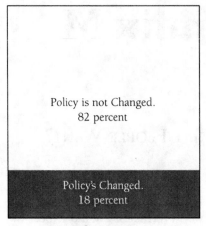

Policy is not Changed.
82 percent

Policy's Changed.
18 percent

Policy is not Changed.
49 percent

Policy's Changed.
51 percent

Opinion favors status quo.
(125 cases)

Opinion favors by change.
(202 cases)

Figure 1 Relationship Between Majority Opinion and Policy Outcomes for 327 cases, 1960–1980. The darker color denotes inconsistencies between policy and opinion. (Source: Alan D. Monroe, "Does the U.S. Government Do What the People Want? [Paper delivered at the Arts and Sciences Lecture, Illinois State University, Normal 26 October 1987], table 2.)

The other major study proceeded somewhat differently. Benjamin Page and Robert Shapiro pored over thousands of questions asked in national surveys between 1935 and 1979, looking for cases of opinion change. They found 231 instances when opinion moved up or down at least 6 percentage points between two surveys *and* when government policy changed in keeping with opinion. Their study—done independently of Monroe's, covering a longer period, and with different objectives—produced a similiar finding: Policy changes were consistent with opinion changes in 66 percent of the cases. Looking at it the other way, policies changed contrary to opinions 34 percent of the time. (Remember, about a 50–50 split would be expected by chance anyway.)

Is there enough congruence between public opinion and policymaking to validate the United States' claim to be a democracy? To approach an answer, we have to examine these two studies more closely. When Page and Shapiro calculated consistency between opinion change and policy change for different levels of opinion change, they found that very large changes in public opinion (20 points or more) produced consistent policy changes more than 90 percent of the time. This suggests that the government responds to major shifts of opinion. Moreover, the authors defend the rationality of the opinion shifts: "When opinion shifts occurred, they were not random or capricious, they were usually related to important changes in citizens' social and economic environment."

To learn which policy areas showed more consistency between public opinion and government action, Monroe analyzed his cases by issue type. He found that consistency was greatest on foreign policy issues and least on issues of political reform. He explained that foreign policy is most nearly under the control of the executive and that the public is more apt to accept presidential leadership in foreign rather than domestic affairs. In contrast, issues of political reform—by definition—require policy change, and many reforms—such as abolishing the electoral college or lowering the voting age—require adoption of a constitutional amendment. Monroe concluded that the most important finding from his data is the bias against change in our political process:

> An all too typical pattern is for the President to propose some new program which enjoys public support and is favorably received by Congressional leaders, but the bill then languishes in committee, passes one house, but not the other, and is eventually rendered irrelevant by the passage of time. It is not that political leaders are not inclined to favor the same positions as public majorities, for they are. The difficulty lies with the complexity of the institutional structure of both Congress and the bureaucracy, the political power of those representing minority positions, and the effects of lobbying by organized groups.

We could argue that government officials should lead rather than follow public opinion. When the U.S. Navy accidentally shot down a civilian Iranian airplane in the Persian Gulf in July 1988 killing 290 passengers, a quick poll found Americans opposed to paying compensation to the victims' families, 49 to 36 percent. Yet President Reagan later announced that the United States would compensate the families. Clearly the president was acting against public opinion. Even if you accept his actions and reject the idea that government should always respond to public opinion, are you satisfied with government that responds to public opinion only about 65 percent of the time?

Monroe believes—as do Page and Shapiro—that the quality of government in America would improve if public opinion played a more important role, if government became more majoritarian. Monroe in particular thinks that stronger political parties—in line with the responsible party model described in Chapter 8—are the key to making the government more majoritarian. But you should not accept what they (or we) believe is the better model of democracy. You must think through what *you* know about American government and politics—about the relationships among freedom, order, and equality and about alternative models of democratic government—and formulate your own views as you grapple with the challenge of democracy.

As we said at the beginning of this book, good government often means making tough choices. By looking beyond specifics to underlying normative principles, you should be able to identify these choices and thus make more sense out of politics. As the years pass and the facts fade (perhaps after the final examination in this course), you should still be able to understand politics by focusing on the underlying conflicts among freedom, order, and equality. Questions about democracy—whether and how to change it—can be interpreted through the majoritarian and pluralist models. Armed with these five key concepts—freedom, order, equality, majoritarianism, and pluralism—you will be better prepared to make political choices. The direction of American government rests in your hands.

 # **Bibliography**

Almond, Gabriel, Bingham Powell, et al., *Comparative Politics: A Theoretical Framework,* Longman/Pearson, 4th ed., 2003.

Berlin, Sir Isaiah, *Two Concepts of Liberty,* Inaugural Lecture as Chichele Professor of Social and Political Theory, Oxford, Clarendon Press, 1958.

Edwards, Wattenberg and Lineberry, *Government in America: People, Politics, and Policy,* Twelfth Edition, Pearson/Longman, 2008.

Friedman, Milton and Rose, *Free to Choose: A Personal Statement,* Harcourt, 1990.

Fulghum, Robert, *All I Really Need To Know I Learned in Kindergarten,* Ballantine Books, 2004.

Lowi, Ginsberg, and Weir, *We the People: An Introduction to American Politics,* Norton, 6th edition, 2007.

Lowi, Theodore, *The End of Liberalism: The Second Republic of the United States.* New York, Norton, 1979.